TRUTH OF SOUL

Truth of Soul

Tadataka Kimura

AuthorHouse™
1663 Liberty Drive
Bloomington, IN 47403
www.authorhouse.com
Phone: 1-800-839-8640

© 2011 by Tadataka Kimura. All rights reserved.

No part of this book may be reproduced, stored in a retrieval system, or transmitted by any means without the written permission of the author.

First published by AuthorHouse   09/30/2011

ISBN: 978-1-4670-0712-2 (sc)
ISBN: 978-1-4670-0711-5 (hc)
ISBN: 978-1-4670-0733-7 (ebk)

Printed in the United States of America

Any people depicted in stock imagery provided by Thinkstock are models, and such images are being used for illustrative purposes only.
Certain stock imagery © Thinkstock.

This book is printed on acid-free paper.

Because of the dynamic nature of the Internet, any web addresses or links contained in this book may have changed since publication and may no longer be valid. The views expressed in this work are solely those of the author and do not necessarily reflect the views of the publisher, and the publisher hereby disclaims any responsibility for them.

Preface

Socrates defined philosophy as "the study of dying," and he considered a person of fifty years of age the most appropriate to take it up. But the study of dying is also the study of life, and the study of what follows death. When I reached fifty years of age, I decided to return to issues that I had explored in my twenties. While I did not call is "philosophy," I examined aspects of the after-death world, the existence of the spiritual body and a scientific way of viewing its structure, the function of the real I (photons), which has its place in the depths of the human psyche and plays the main role in it, and the universal laws governing the soul in relation to various religions and sciences.

This book will breathe life into the modern way of looking at the issue of the truth of the soul. It will renew the debate and proposes a new way of viewing what it means to be human. It aims to release the mind from its fetters, which have limited and deluded people for many thousands of years.

I am only an ordinary doctor; I do not belong to any religion or faction or organisation. I have written this book through my own clinical experiences within the scope of internal medicine, emergency medicine, and psychiatric and psychosomatic medicine. I have immersed myself in the works of splendid wise men of the past. Since my youth I have had the privilege of meeting many monks and mediums.

All truths, until they were recognised and unanimously accepted, were mocked, and their purveyors were slandered and despised. This is particularly true when dealing with the spiritual world.

The Bible tells us that "there is nothing new under the Sun" (Ecclesiastes 1:9). And indeed, this book is nothing more than a form that expresses in modern language the ideas of those who sacrificed their efforts and even lives to express them. I undertook the attempt to shed some scientific light on the truth hidden deep inside the psyche. In order not to lose our precious spiritual heritage, I decided to employ language the modern reader could understand, avoiding, whenever it was possible, religious expressions.

I wish to convince the Reader that, living in the world divided by our five senses, we do not comprehend, just like creatures living in water know nothing about the ground, that in different frequencies, surprisingly many other worlds coexists in parallel to our own, and I would be very glad if I could revolutionise a present view on a man and his consciousness.

At the beginning of this book, I explain the space origin of our bodies, the way they were being shaped through the evolution of space matter, and then I present the evolution of life on the Earth.

Next, using modern scientific techniques, I demonstrate that our bodies are subject to electromagnetic forces that radiate with energy.

Further, I try to explain that issues presented above were defined by the language of religion as "the truth in the depth of psyche", while I identify them with the real I (photons) and describe in detail its functions.

Those who do not want to acknowledge the existence of the spiritual world will criticise my inability to present unequivocal scientific proof that it exists. Obviously, there is also no scientific proof that it does not exist. It is not the role of science to explore such matters, but both scientists and ordinary people should follow good manners and stop themselves from passing negative judgement.

Even if this work includes some mistakes or minor faults, I am convinced that I can capture the whole essence of this matter, and that is why I have decided to probe the subject of the existence of the soul, to look from a scientific point of view at the structure of the spiritual body, and finally to describe it without hesitation.

This subject is always met with prejudice or mocking, but in fact this "science of dying" is also the "science of life" and is closely related to our everyday lives, for sooner or later we will meet a physical death.

I discuss in detail forces of evil, which exist in our world as well as in the world of spirits, for in my opinion it is extremely crucial to understand their misdeeds and their influence.

The psyche is our own work of art. Proceeding from this assumption, I show how the psyche influences joy, which derives from its essence and its productiveness. The development of the psyche enables the evolution and perfection of the soul.

If the essence of true religion is the understanding of pure love, some religious doctrines do not function well, especially in the modern world, where it is difficult to distinguish what is valuable and what is not. Moreover, many religions actually inhibit the development of the psyche by making man dependent and stopping him at the level of being immature. At the same time, he is exposed to various dilemmas of this world, which are the result of diversity of faith systems and conflicts resulting from different hierarchies of values.

In this book, I try to discuss the quintessence of religion without applying its specific vocabulary and to explain anomalies of faith systems and spiritual mechanisms created by religion. I also make the attempt to discover the direction man should follow to soar at the highest level of consciousness and be able to develop psychically. Truly mastering the psyche enables us to manifest the true "I".

If holy books and doctrines have any mainspring in the future, they will have to embrace respect and devotion to life as their main goals. Taking this position as the starting point, they will be able to explore universal rights governing the soul, changing words, faith, deeds, and the consciousness of man.

I will be glad, if this book helps my readers, at least a bit, to discover a new understanding of man and his "ego".

CONTENTS

Chapter I The psyche, the body, and electromagnetic waves . 1
   1. The body, which contains the space 1
   2. Bioplasm 4
   3. Electromagnetic waves 6
   4. Matter and energy 10
   5. Electromagnetic waves emitted by the body 13
   6. Activity of the brain and electromagnetic waves ... 16
   7. Electronic memory 19
   8. Psyche and matter 20

Chapter II The spiritual body and the world of spirits 23
   1. The origin of the spiritual body
      and its structure from a scientific point of view 23
   2. About the origin of the world of spirits
      and factors dividing it 30

Chapter III Functions of the real I (photons) 35

Chapter IV Waves of the soul, the world of spirits,
   and its class society 43
   1. What are waves of the soul? 43
   2. The world of spirits and the class structure
      of its society 44
   3. Egoism world 49
   4. The world of good people 50
   5. The world of bright intelligence 51
   6. The world of Bodhisattva 52

  7. The world of Buddha 53
  8. Heaven 54

Chapter V Incarnation and incarnated spirits 59

Chapter VI Behaviour models of evil spirits 61

Chapter VII Possession 65

Chapter VIII Guarding spirits and guiding spirits 67

Chapter IX Parapsychology and
parapsychological abilities 69

Chapter X What is the obstacle to
correct understanding? 72

  1. Negative results of religions: Islam, Judaism,
    Christianity, and Buddhism. 72
  2. Negative results of ideologies and dogmas 93
  3. Properties of functions of the brain 95
  4. Mechanisms of psyche and defence mechanisms ... 96

Chapter XI Personality disorders 98

Chapter XII About Joy 101

Chapter XIII The unity of everything 104

Chapter XIV Soul perfection 106

Chapter XV Holy books and their future 112

Conclusion 119

Bibliography 120

CHAPTER I
THE PSYCHE, THE BODY, AND ELECTROMAGNETIC WAVES

1. THE BODY, WHICH CONTAINS THE SPACE

Approximately 60 billion cells constitute the human body. They are divided into twenty types. The variety of cells is a result of the fact that each particular type, serving a different function, is formed by a specific set of genes. Every day, around 300 million cells divide, meaning that every seven years, all cells of the human body are new.

The cells of the human body are connected with complicated dependencies and together fulfil one function. At the same time, functions of particular cells are part of one whole, whose functioning is supervised by the central organ that unites everything in our organism—the brain. Our cells operate without a single break, keeping the harmony between each organ's role and the benefit of the whole organism.

The following non-organic minerals can be found in the human body: sodium (Na), potassium (K), chlorine (Cl), calcium (Ca), phosphorus (P), iron (Fe), iodine (I), mercury (Hg), fluorine (F), nickel (Ni), cadmium (Cd), and zinc (Zn). Each of these minerals fulfils an important physiological function. Particularly important are sodium, potassium, and chlorine, which are electrolytic elements that take part in generating voltage and achieving the acid-base balance. Minerals such as magnesium (Mg) and iron (Fe) support transport of coenzymes and oxygen (O_2), while others, such as calcium (Ca) and zinc (Zn), take part in the secretion of hormones. Every major deviation from the correct concentration of particular minerals in the blood poses a threat to life: our bodies are engaged in an endless fight to keep the right levels of these minerals.

The latest research in astrophysics points to a surprising truth about the origin of the above-mentioned elements and the evolution of matter. It states that atoms of oxygen (O) and atoms of carbon (C), which are found in our bodies, came into being inside remote stars that ended their lives billions years ago. It means that the matter of which our bodies are made is nothing more than crumbs of stars.

I will explain this more simply below:

Stars shine due to energy, which is released as a result of thermonuclear reactions inside them. An essential fuel for such a reaction is hydrogen gas. As a result, hydrogen (H) turns into helium (He), which in a chain reaction turns into heavy elements (hydrogen H → helium He → carbon C → nitrogen N → oxygen O → neon Ne → sodium Na → magnesium Mg → silicon Si → iron Fe), releasing their nuclear energy simultaneously.

However, as the weight of a star is limited, its fuel is also limited.

After the stages H → He → C of the thermonuclear reaction, a star whose weight is similar to that of the Sun will turn into a red giant.[1] The Sun, which heats the Earth, will expand so much within 5 billion years that Mercury and Venus will be engulfed and the Sun will get closer to the Earth. Its middle part will turn

---

[1] Red giant—a star at the end stage of its evolution.

into a white dwarf[2], start to cool down, and decrease to the size of our planet.

In the case of a star with a weight eight times that of the Sun, a thermonuclear reaction will pass through the stages H → He → C → N → O → Si → Fe, until the star is not able to bear its own weight and causes the explosion of a supernova. During such an explosion, the maximum degree of intensity of light is 100 million times greater than the light emitted by the Sun. It can be compared to the degree of intensity of the whole light emitted by the Milky Way. In such a moment, elements such as carbon (C), nitrogen (N), oxygen (O), and iron (Fe) are created in a thermonuclear reaction, along with all the other elements that originated due to the high temperature and energy of the explosion itself, and they are ejected into space.

When space began, the only existing elements were hydrogen (H) and helium (He). Heavy elements were not present, but due to the explosion of a supernova, they are found in the interstellar centre. The age of a small star is one billion years, while the age of a star similar to the Sun is 10 milliard years, for stars of a greater weight it is 100 million years, and for those, whose mass is enormous, age is c. one million years.

All elements of which our bodies, as well as our planet, are built were subjected to a thermonuclear reaction in a reactor that was a star of a huge mass a long time ago, and then, with then explosion of a supernova, they were spread throughout Milky Way. So we can say that, just as a memory about the development and evolution of life is written in DNA, it is we who contain the matter from the space. We became creatures who have consciousness and the ability to create and at the same time are influenced by the powerful rhythm of nature.

---

[2] White dwarf—a small (approximately the size of the Earth) astronomical object releasing a white light.

2. Bioplasm

Life on Earth is completely dependent on solar energy, which reaches our planet in the form of electromagnetic waves (light). The human body is being kept alive due to the work of 60 billion cells. It is almost scientifically proven that energy released during the cellular work turns into light and is sent beyond the body. Energy may be referred to as biophotons, bioplasm, bioenergy, or aura. I would to say a few words about the history of its discovery and about its essence.

In 1923, the Russian biologist Alexander Gurwitsch was the first person to discover that the human body sends photons in the form of an electromagnetic wave; he named them "biophotons". Not until 1974 did the scientist Fritz Albert Popp prove the existence of biophotons and measure their emission frequency.

The shape and colour of a human aura alters with thoughts and emotions. Photographs called Kirlian photographs of a person's aura can be used to estimate the state of health of that person. Kirlian photography is named for a Soviet electrotechnician, Siemion Kirlian, who in 1950 processed an object placed on photographic film by using an electrical impulse of frequency from 75 thousand to 200 thousand per second released by a power generator of great frequency. This allowed him to take a picture without the use of a camera.

Later, Dr Walter John Kilner created a "Kilner screen" covered with a dicyanate solution to prove that there are three radiating layers of aura surrounding the human body. A few years earlier, a group of Russian scientists had declared, "We discovered that a body of living organism sends vibrations of energy of frequency from 300 to 2000 nanometres," calling this energy a "biofield" or "bioplasm". So the phenomenon called Life energy[3] in Chinese philosophy or Prana[4] in Hinduism, or depicted as a halo surrounding sculptured images of buddhas or gold aureoles above the heads of angels in Christian art, is actually bioplasma, aura, and biophotons.

The suffix "-plasm" means a gas, which contains electrically charged particles and originated due to ionisation. In the natural world, these participles move hydro-dynamically like gases or liquids. Tiny, electrically charged particles moving in a large concentration are usually called plasma, and physicists believe that it is a state between energy and matter.

Sometimes at a particular frequency of vibration, this energetic bioplasm gives a heat effect that we can see. This heat vibrates and shines brightly around the living organism, and is a glowing field that not only surrounds the body, yet also infiltrates it. Man is not only a physical being, but also a being capable of releasing light. This light cannot be observed with the naked eye and depends on the states of mind and body, for we can observe changes in the colour and shape of this light.

The human body also has its own particular frequency, which results from the frequency of particular cells, while differences in frequencies are visibly manifested by changes in colour. Attempts were undertaken to change frequencies specific to particular cells (of the brain, heart, etc.) into colours and to use them in a therapy (chromotherapy).

Plasma changes its colour, shape, and intensity of light under the influence of emotional states, thoughts, and consciousness, while cells release their own colours and energy, which are sent

---

[3] Life energy—Energy circulating in the human body and keeping it healthy (*ki, qi, chi*)
[4] Prana—The life power, which keeps all creatures alive and is identified with a breath.

beyond the body in the form of light. Inside the body there is an informational net, formed by biophotons or bioplasm, which is used to send and receive information, forming a living system for communication and information.

3. ELECTROMAGNETIC WAVES

Let us now consider light, or electromagnetic waves, with respect to modern quantum mechanics. This light forms our bodies, our psyches, and—going further—the whole matter and beginning of space. What is more, life on Earth is completely dependent on solar energy, which is the form in which light reaches us by means of electromagnetic waves.

Light is electromagnetic waves, called by various names depending on their frequency. Electromagnetic waves originate due to the cooperation of the electric field and the magnetic field. The double nature of light, which joins particles with a wave, is characteristic for all electromagnetic waves. Putting it simply, light is a wave whose speed allows it to encircle the Earth 7.5 times per second, and during a year to travel a distance of 9.5 billion kilometres.

Along with the change of long, medium, and short radio waves into ultra—short FM, or in the case of television waves, VHF, their frequency grows. A frequency of terahertz waves is even higher. These waves are used to examine interiors of objects, without the necessity to open them and to check a structure of particular substances. Lately they are used to recognise fingerprints or monitor security threats, or diagnose cancerous tumours.

Even faster vibrating waves are rays of far infrared and visible light. Cells of the human retina are able to catch electromagnetic waves of length equal to between 0.0004 and 0.0008 millimetres. Electromagnetic waves within these limits are possible to see, which is why they are defined as "visible" in this narrow meaning.

The next waves are ultraviolet rays, X-rays, and gamma rays. The latter are used for radiotherapy and to remove tumour foci, wherein the length of their wave is less than 0.1nm (1nm = 0.000001mm), and their frequency is 10^{18} Hz (this unit of frequency indicates the number of vibrations per second). It means that gamma waves are electromagnetic waves, and it is hard to believe that the number of vibrations is equal to one million billion times per second, for it exceeds the limits of our comprehension.

All waves mentioned above are generally called electromagnetic waves or light (in the broader sense of this word). They are all characterised by basic vibrations, just like light and photons, which is why they can be collectively called "light".

We cannot see or feel with our other senses any electromagnetic waves apart from visible light, until they are used in such devices as radios, televisions, short-wave transmitters, microwaves, mobile phones or satellite navigation, and we can see how they reach us turned into images, words, or music. We cannot deny their existence because they are "invisible".

When the space probe Cassini-Huygens, sent by the American National Aeronautics and Space Administration (NASA), after seven years reached the orbit of Saturn, it sent pictures of this planet, its rings, and its moons, and we were able to see them due to electromagnetic waves.

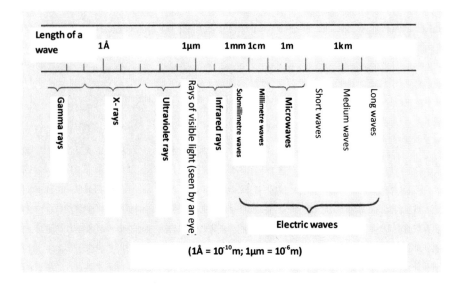

Fig. 1-1

Figure 1-1 shows the lengths of waves and types of electromagnetic waves. Not only light (visible light), but also gamma radiation, X—rays, ultraviolet rays, infrared rays, and electric waves are types of "electromagnetic waves" that move in the space. A distance between successive crests is called the length of the wave, while "frequency" is the number of waves per second. All electromagnetic waves move with the same speed, 300 thousand kilometres per second. Therefore, there is a relationship between the length of a wave and its frequency:

[length of a wave] × [frequency] = [speed of an electromagnetic wave] = [speed of light]

When the length of a wave is longer, its frequency and energy are lower. In Figure 1-1, the length of an electromagnetic wave grows (and its frequency is lower) as we move to the right. The length of the wave and its frequency determine the differences between electromagnetic waves.

Only 1 per cent of electromagnetic waves in space are produced by stars; the other 99 percent is light called "microwave background radiation", which originated during the first stages of the evolution of space, long before the birth of stars. At the beginning, space was a soup of heavy light in which a bit of matter was mixed (nuclei and electrons of hydrogen and helium). Per each 1 m³ there were approximately 400 thousand photons of microwave background radiation, while the number of atoms forming the matter of all of space did not exceed 10 / 1m³. Despite their enormous numbers, single photons contained very little energy, which is why when photon energy was collected in the form of light from all of space, it would only be equal to 10^{-5} weight of all matter. All astronomical objects are like fish, splashing in a sea of electromagnetic waves.

We are able to see only 4 per cent of space matter. Twenty-three per cent of space is made up of dark matter (it is believed that dark matter, which occurs very irregularly in space, is a type of stellar cemetery, which concentrates residues of supernova explosions occurring in various parts of space; it may also consist of dwarfs in their decadent form), and the remaining 73 per cent is the energy of a vacuum. We have explored only 4 per cent of space matter, and we know nothing about 90 per cent.

However, electromagnetic waves allow us to understand one crucial fact: differences in frequencies cause changes in the amount of energy, its properties, colour, and function. This means that it is frequency that defines matter. Vibrations determine its existence and temperature, the intensity of its light, and its properties and colour.

Let us consider the relation between frequency of vibrations, the psyche, and matter.

4. MATTER AND ENERGY

When vibrations of energy waves (light) find in their path a proper medium, there is a change due to which they transmit themselves into the world of large vibrations. Such media are elementary particles, such as electrons and mesons.

Sometimes elementary particles originate from energy, and sometimes they create the energy. Incredibly huge energy joins, overlaps, adheres to itself, and crystallises. Then its frequency falls and this is how the matter is born. That is why matter is comprised of pure energy; we can state that it is energy that simply was stopped or crystallised.

A thought, which is the result of the work of the brain, is pure, electromagnetic vibration of energy. If we follow the logic in Figure 1-2, we see that it is possible to give a material form to it. When a large amount of energy moves, matter is created. The matter is comprised of joined and crystallised vibrations of energy, which still move around. In this way, the matter is formed from pure vibrations of energy. What is more, it can originate only in this way.

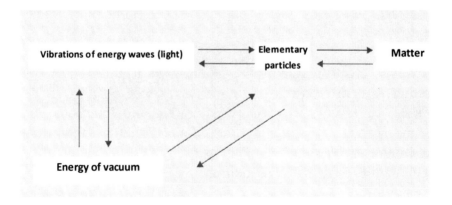

Fig. 1-2

Quantum Field Theory states that elementary particles are described by vibrations of a field. The space (vacuum) is filled by a "field". It is assumed that this field is subject to vibrations. As a result, particles spread from a vacuum. That is why elementary particles are described as vibrations of a field. Strong waving of a field means that there is too much energy, which originates in the state when elementary particles exist; when energy disappears, the field stops vibrating and there are no elementary particles. The state in which vibrations stops is defined as a vacuum.

When energy is turned into matter, it remains in this form until it is destroyed by reversed or different energy.

Albert Einstein said that "mass is equal to energy and they can mutually transform." We can formulate a similar statement: Thoughts, emotions, and consciousness, which are energy produced by the brain (by mental work), are equal to a particular matter whose frequency is similar.

The whole universe vibrates and all beings are defined by frequencies. Each sends its own frequency and has waves that are specific to it, which cross and disturb each other.

The universe is like a symphonic work played by an enormous number of vibrations. That is why all included elements are created from vibrating energy and waves.

We live at the matter level of a very low frequency; that is why it is hard for us to understand elementary particles and waves. The notions of atom, electron, or particle are of only symbolic meaning to us, for they were introduced first and foremost to facilitate an integrated description of the whole phenomenon. In spite of the fact that matter is made up of many elementary particles, these particles are too abstract to call them "matter".

If we look at this issue from the point of view of light, especially in the way it is presented in the last picture, surely we will understand that everything existing in the universe was formed due to transformations of light.

According to the Holy Book, at the beginning there was light. Everything existing in the universe was created due to the transformation of light. Let us remember that in this way everything was formed, and not only visible light. The basis for action in the universe is its beginning, light, and when photon (spin ①) turns into two antiphotons (spin ① and spin ②), then each of the separated photons and antiphotons experiences the following transformation:

And further, repeating processes of division and connection, photons and antiphotons created everything we can see and touch. So, the surrounding world is only a composition of waves (it is the content and actions of light), which took on various shapes. When two waves cross and disturb each other, they adopt a form of various shapes and colours. We can state that colour is a "secondary" wave, which reflects the content and actions of a primary wave. That is why colour—the course of its synthesis or division and also the way it changes—lets us know the actions and functions of the wave from which it originated.

I have been writing so far that everything existing in the universe was created from vibrating energy (waves), and this thought is developed in "superstring theory", which is an important theory of modern theoretical physics. I am going to explain it briefly:

— Matter consists of atoms and atoms are made of quarks and electrons. In fact, all these particles form vibrating strings bent into a circle. A typical circle is a size very close to the Planck length (c. 10^{-55}cm).

— The resonant frequency of a string determines its mass, the charge of its force, and the properties of its elementary particles, while the length of a wave and its vibrations determine the amount of its energy.

— Energy is stronger when the length of a wave is shorter and its amplitude is larger.

— According to this theory, the value of 10^{-55} cm and the shape of the vibrations of the smallest circle of a string decide the whole matter and energy.

The particles do not form points, but schemas of wave vibrations. It is possible for psychogenic energy, in the form of thought and consciousness, to form the world and its physical environment by acting on matter from the region of a similar frequency. There is a world that obtains shapes by the cooperation of the psyche with matter. So, can regions of various frequencies, especially the high ones which cannot be seen by the human eye, be called the world of spirits?

5. ELECTROMAGNETIC WAVES EMITTED BY THE BODY

In the central part of the brain, just behind the eyes and above the line separating the brain hemispheres, there is an organ of internal secretion (it secrets melatonin and serotonin) whose shape resembles a pine cone. It is called the pineal gland. The pineal gland, whose photosensitive protein resembles the protein (opsins) in the retina, originally was extremely photosensitive and reacted to light, and has many features in common with the organ of sight. It is sometimes called the "third eye".

The pineal gland became an internal organ in mammals, and almost all people lost its photosensitive functions. It was called by the ancients "Epiphysis", which means awakening. In the Hindu yoga system, it is recognised as Ajna chakra, and it was defined by René Descartes, exploring spirituality, as "the throne of the soul".

It is suggested that continuously submitting the pineal gland and diencephalon to particular stimuli allows it to adjust to the greater number of electromagnetic waves, allowing something usually unnoticed to be visible. The meditation practice *Fugen-bosatsu gumonji-hō*[5], which was performed by the Japanese monk Kūkai[6] on a Muroto-misaki cape, is an example of a ritual that in a continuous way directed all stimuli to the pineal gland and diencephalon.

There are many worlds formed by large vibrations of low frequency, which comprise the sphere in which we live, to the world of tiny vibrations of high frequency. It is obvious that creatures existing in the band of large vibrations do not see the world of high frequencies. It is this band of high frequencies that is usually called "the other world" or "the world of spirits".

In each area of vibrations, there is one world, one universe.

---

[5] *Fugen-bosatsu gumonji-hō*—A Buddhist meditation practice called "mediation of the morning star'. It is assumed as a method of perfecting the mind and the ability to reason.

[6] Kūkai (774-835)—The Japanese monk, scholar, poet, and artist, founder of the Buddhist sect Shingon.

Suppose that there is a world whose frequency was increased. For people who live in the primary frequency of this world, it becomes invisible, and because frequency of the matter surrounding them increases, people in the world of a higher frequency may not only see such matter, yet also touch it and lead their previous lives. Changes in frequency allow for sudden disappearing and appearing, and even can cause changes in the space-time continuum. That is why, apart from the world that we can see and touch, there are also worlds that overlap on ours or adjoin it.

In the worlds of high frequencies, the mental-work-waves sphere and material-waves sphere, which shape the environment, are quite similar; that is why it seems to be possible to create the environment and the world with the energy of thoughts and consciousness. Being conscious and thinking means producing vibrations of energy of a great speed, which, when it collides and joins with a huge charge of similar energy, increases its weight and decreases its frequency, to form finally a material being and environment made of it. I must add that thought waves are believed to reach a frequency of 5 millimetres (60 GHz), so if it was possible to send electronic information, knowledge, and human thoughts in this band in a continuous way, it would be possible to transmit them in a very short period of time. It would also prove the existence of telepathy.

Our bodies have an established frequency related very closely to the frequencies of particular cells. As I have already mentioned, differences in frequencies are expressed in changes of colour, and it is possible to know interactions of frequencies themselves by observing them. Energy released during cellular work is sent beyond the body in the form of light, which we call biophotons or bioplasm. Inside the body there is an informational net made of biophotons, which emits energy in all directions. Remember, frequencies sent by us are subject to constant change, due to thoughts, moods, and emotions.

Therefore we can assume that astrology is a credible field, which takes the moment of birth of a man as its starting point and predicts his fate based on the idea that the mutual distortions and cooperation of electromagnetic energy sent by the human body with electromagnetic waves that are changed by each movement of the celestial bodies decide that fate.

6. ACTIVITY OF THE BRAIN AND ELECTROMAGNETIC WAVES

Let us consider functions and electromagnetic activities of the brain, which is the central organ in the human body. Nerve cells in the brain work (producing emotions and thoughts) due to the action current that is produced in the nervous system, and thought and brain waves operating in the frequency band of c. 5 mm (60 GHz) are together released. A Motionless Electromagnetic Generator (MEG), which measures changes in the magnetic field caused by the work of the brain, has lately been used in the diagnosis of diseases and for studies of brain operations.

It is already known that in both the brain and the heart, there are electric waves. When voltage is produced inside the body, current flows through it, indicating lines of magnetic forces. These lines have a charge of only 10^{-6} of the charge of the geomagnetism. So far it has been difficult to measure that charge, yet due to the progress in electronic technologies it has become possible to measure the lines of magnetic forces originating in the brain and heart. A record of this measurement is called a magneto-cardiogram.

A device that creates an image using magnetic resonance, a Magnetic Resonance Imaging, or MRI, determines the distribution of electric-wave energy produced in the human body by placing a person inside the device, where extremely strong magnetic interactions are generated. Use of a superconducting magnet in an MRI machine allows it to catch, in the form of a three-dimensional image, the slightest anomalies in the brain and other organs. This makes the diagnosis process easier. In this way, electromagnetic interactions connected with the human body are being discovered.

In spite of the fact that the brain accounts for only 2 per cent of the weight of an adult man, it uses 18 per cent of the energy. The only source of this energy is glucose, with which, just like oxygen, the brain must be supplied. The brain receives 15 to 16 per cent of the blood being pumped by the heart, and 20 per cent of the body's supply of oxygen is burnt by this organ. The huge amounts of oxygen and energy used by the brain are the proof of its rapid metabolism.

The evolution of a single cell started 3.5 milliard years ago, and 600 million years ago cells began to join with each other, forming multicellular organisms. Complex life could not function and survive unless particular cells communicated with each other about their state and reactions. Nerves provide the intercellular information net. At the beginning, they fulfilled the very simple function of quickly passing information about stimuli, but after some time, their abilities became more complex. Although it still reacted to information immediately, some part of the nervous system started to collect such information and memorise it. Over time, this part learnt to transform all gathered information and finally developed into the highly organised human brain.

Basically, the brain of vertebrates consists of three parts: the brain stem, the cerebellum, and the brain. This structure is the same for all species, but there are substantial differences in the relative sizes of particular parts. The brain sustains its basic structure but evolves by increasing particular parts. In the case of humans, this took the form of substantial growth of the prefrontal cortex.

Cells of the brain form a huge net. In all parts of the brain together, there are 100 milliard of them. In the telencephalon, there are 20 milliard, or around 100 thousand of cells per 1mm^3. If we could connect all nerve-cell dendrites, they would spread for one million kilometres, and they form a huge system in which one nervous cell is connected to 10 thousand others. Nervous cells are specific cells that send electric signals to exchange information, yet they are not tightly connected with each other and tiny spaces can be found between them.

In the synaptic cleft, which connects nerves and transforms an electrical signal into a chemical one, neurotransmitters are used. So far, several types of neurotransmitters and neuromodulators have been discovered, including noradrenalin, dopamine, and serotonin. When action potential reaches the end of a cell, a neurotransmitter is secreted, which turns an electrical signal into a chemical one in a synapse, and information is further transmitted.

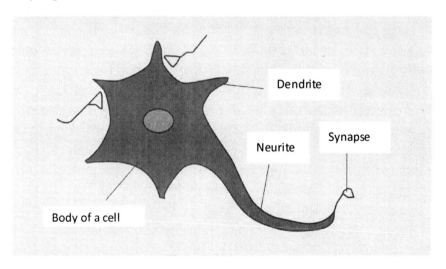

Fig. 1-3 Nervous cell

In various neurons (nervous units consisting of the body of a cell, neurite, and dendrites) there are various receptors and neurotransmitters that are secreted by them. For this reason, the distinctness of a single neurotransmitter and receptor means the distinctness of the brain function and the work of the heart. The incorrect number of neurotransmitters and receptors, or distortions of their sensitivity, may cause many psychical and behavioural disorders.

In the nervous system, the action current is produced. This current allows thoughts and emotions to be born. The brain may be compared to a great electric circuit where electromagnetic forces direct our thoughts and memory. Recorded in its memory are changes of electromagnetic waves sent by a human under the influence of his thoughts, moods, and actions.

7. Electronic Memory

The memory mechanism stores information and is connected to functions of the spiritual body. Within the human body, the brain and peripheral nerves transmit, collect and remember information through electromagnetic (electric) signals, while electromagnetic waves are used as transmitters of information in our close environment. They are found in radios, TV sets, mobile phones, and satellite navigation, as well as in space probes and weapons. Initially, magnetic tapes were used as carriers for collection and storage of information, yet with increasing amount of recorded information, they were replaced with floppy disks, and then with compact disks (CD), mini disks (MD), and DVD disks. All these carriers act following the same principle, which turns image, music, letters, etc., into digital signal (0, 1), records it, and then sends it. At present, taking a very simplified division, there are three methods of recording a digital signal:

— Method using magnetism (floppy disks)

— Method using light (CD, DVD)

— Method using electrons (flash memory)

Semiconductors use the third method and, depending on the situation, they can conduct or not conduct current. This structure allows them to extend or insert electrons inside them with changes of voltage. Similarly, the spiritual body is an electro-ionic plasm in the form of a gas. It is believed to have obtained a self-organising function of remembering and thinking, and is therefore closest to the method of transmission and recording of information by use of electrons.

8. Psyche and matter

When we observe crystals of snow, unquestionably we are charmed with the perfection of their patterns and their elaborate and symmetric structure. Everyone at least once has had a moment when, looking at stars shining in the night sky, they have felt that in their beautiful and dignified movement there is a kind of intervention of something rational. Faced with the harmony, multicolours, and artistic character of nature, or thinking about the perfected and rational mechanism of life, everyone has at some time felt fright filled with respect and admiration for how everything functions logically.

Einstein wrote once: *When I stay in the face of a perfect harmony in which the nature operates, I am filled with such emotion, which is a kind of religious ecstasy. In such moment, I can only admire the perfection of this intelligence, and all thoughts and actions, in which the mankind has participated so far, seem to be only pathetic effort.*

When ultrasonic waves work on one type of virus, especially over the four proteins of which it is made, they break down, yet if they are left in such state, they connect once again into their initial integrity. This phenomenon is called "the self-organising system". The same name is used to define the tendency of nature to reach symmetrical forms, an example of which is the spherical shape.

We know that the human body consists of proteins, which are formed by the DNA junction of four basic elements with twenty types of amino acids. Thus are complex structures inside living organisms formed.

Such a self-organising system is evident in detail in the case of proteins. Even at the level of non-organic nanoparticiples (nanometre means the value equal to 10^{-9} m), the self-organising of elaborate structures has been observed.

A report was published in the October 2006 journal *Science* suggesting that "the driving force of self-organising systems is hydrophobic cooperation (the tendency to push particles of water) or electrostatic cooperation between particles."

On the basis of these facts, we can state that life and nature hide intelligent and wise interactions in themselves, which form elaborate structures of organisms and shape their functions. The forces of our modern science are not equal to such interactions. We use only a part of wisdom, which is hidden in life and nature.

In nature, in life, and in matter itself, there is a psychogenic interaction, which is a force aiming at sustaining harmony, balance, and order, without which evolution would not have a reason to exist. Therefore we can state that both in matter and in living organisms, starting from elementary particles, through molecules, and ending at cells, there is wisdom, which orders them and leads to evolution. This suggests a psychogenic element of matter, whose interaction would not have existed without it as the base.

Psychogenic and physical interactions work together, and they cannot function separately. We have a tendency to consider matter and the psyche as two completely different things, but now, when we realise that psychogenic and physical interactions form an integrated whole, it is extremely crucial for understanding the spiritual body, the world of spirits, and the distinct consciousnesses about which I am concerned.

Chapter II

The Spiritual Body and the World of Spirits

1. The Origin of the Spiritual Body and its Structure from a Scientific Point of View

People see only things that are of the length of waves adjusted to our needs; the scope of our seeing depends on the waves we send. This means that everyone can see according to his own acting. Sight and vision change depending on a person and a situation; therefore one person can see something that it is not possible for another to observe.

For example, usually we can distinguish several dozen of colours, while we can create almost 68 milliard of them. So, there are as many as 68 milliard waves and frequencies, while from the view of electromagnetic waves their number may be infinite. We demand material proof; it is difficult for us to believe in anything until we see it with our own eyes, yet we must be able to understand that we function in a world that is limited by our five senses.

Let us summarize everything discussed so far relating to the spiritual body:

—In addition to the body, which is visible to eyes, man also consists of electromagnetic energy.

— Radiating elements of different frequencies overlap the body.

— It has been proven that light (biophotons) is sent from human cells, and we are able to measure that light.

— There is an informational network in the human body, consisting of biophotons, which transmits electromagnetic signals and transmits information by means of electrons and also has memory.

— Modern devices allow for displaying an aura and biophotons on a screen, while the frequency of shining photons, which are the centre of the spiritual body and are placed in the middle of the human head, and the frequency of the body itself are too high to be visible to an average person, yet a person who is able to adjust to the slightest vibrations of high frequency will see them.

On the basis of scientific discoveries and meta-psychic research conducted by my predecessors, and of the revelations of Saints, I will here make observations and conclusions about the structure and functions of the spiritual body. And in spite of the fact that scientific proof, which would completely confirm this information, has not yet been found, I can still determine the main issue.

1.) The spiritual body as electromagnetic reconstruction of a physical body

In one definition of living organisms, there is the notion of "auto-replication", or self-reconstructing. Similarly to the physical body, which performs auto-replication by means of DNA and RNA, the spiritual body originates due to auto-replication, which can be defined as the electromagnetic reconstruction of the physical body. The flow of a low current through the cerebral cortex transfers information, which, due to electrons flowing through the brain, is transmitted at the same time to the spiritual body. This information is coded and remembered by these electrons. Probably the spiritual body gained the capacity to be transmitted in an electromagnetic way when the stabilisation of the electromagnetic field took place at a constant flow of current. An electromagnetic information network was formed, and electronic memory allowed it to remember and record an enormous amount of information. It can be compared to a photograph taken by a camera, which shows the highly developed electric circuit of the brain and also works like it.

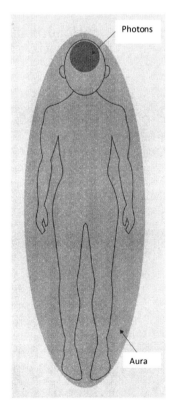

Fig. 2-1. Photons

2.) The spiritual body is magnetically connected with the physical body

A magnetic field and the lines of its force, which produce a low current flowing through the brain, sometimes are blocked or cut. When current stops flowing, the physical body dies, and the spiritual body leaves it.

3.) When a biomagnetic field separates from the brain along with the spiritual body, the former receives particles of air, which can be easily magnetized.

Matter in a natural way aims to create high structures of symmetrical shapes like spherical forms. Probably for this reason, just after death, the spiritual body takes the shape of a sphere with diameter equal to 35 cm. I also must add that the weight of the body is reduced by about 26 grams in the moment of death. After some time, organic substances and all the necessary elements disappear and the spiritual body turns into a plasmatic sphere of a diameter equal to 5 cm, comprised mainly of electrons and elementary particles.

The diameter of this sphere can be changed in any way.

4.) The spiritual body keeps the consciousness, memory, and character formed during the life of the physical body.

The spiritual body has emotions and the capacity to think, just as it did when it had the physical body.

5.) Soon after death of the body, one part, in the form of a jelly-like, fluid plasma, separates from it, and then it turns into a gas plasma.

It is a translucent, shining sphere consisting of a gas.

When the monk Kūkai decided that his meditation practice *Fugen-bosatsu gumonji-hō* on the cape Muroto-misaki was over, he wrote: *"Venus came to me from far away and entered my mouth."* This probably means that a creature from heaven wanted to communicate with the monk and inform him that his practice had ended, and in order to celebrate it, the creature decided to put into his mouth a holy ghost from heaven, or in other words, the spiritual body (an orange sphere). The spiritual body in the shape of the orange sphere could be similar to the morning star.

6.) The spiritual body keeps an outer plasmatic covering or membrane.

7.) Except for cacti, also known as talking plants, and some species of animals and more developed plants, no other counterparts of the spiritual body have been found.

A very likely reason for this fact is the impossibility of rising over physiological shock of death.

8.) During the lifetime, the spiritual body overlaps the physical body.

9.) Due to consciousness exercises, we can turn into shapes and forms that vary from our original ones.

10.) When a fertilized egg starts its cell-division process, at the same time, its electromagnetic copy, or spiritual body, comes into existence.

In both primary beliefs and new religions, there is the conception of some kind of spiritual existence, or spirit of the universe, whose separated part in the form of the soul found shelter in a human being. Yet this is not a correct assumption, for the spiritual body is created with the birth and development of the physical body. Some religions believe that the world of spirits is the real one, while our world and our physical shell are only temporary forms. However, I have seen personally, how, naturally and due to evolution, a living organism is born in a spiritual form, rising above the death of the body. This organism lives and keeps the consciousness of the physical body. It is a very moving experience.

11.) **I would like to repeat at this point that a creature that created a mankind, after reaching the last stage of evolution, which gave man a body with a highly developed structure and functions, in a surprising way overcame the state of shock that death is for the body. It obtained the ability to continue its existence in the modified form of a plasmatic gas sphere of invariably high frequency.**

This is what we call the spiritual body.

12.) **When destructive energy acts on the spiritual body, it is broken into elementary particles.**

This means that the spiritual body does not age and is not threatened by death. Nevertheless it still may die. Unfortunately, it cannot prevail against all types of physical energy.

13.) **The spiritual body may move at a great speed due to its short-wave nature.**

14.) **The spiritual body can consciously change its frequency, decreasing it to the level at which it can be observed** with the naked eye or increasing it in order to disappear suddenly.

15.) Due to the short length of its waves, the spiritual body can walk through glass, walls, or other matter.

It can also freely enter or leave the human body.

16.) The spiritual body can influence human consciousness.

It can influence the consciousness and sense, and it can incite hatred and push the physical body to evil and impulsive deeds.

17.) The spiritual body acts on human senses, allowing it to hear sounds or to see things which usually are beyond of the reach of the man.

It can change real feeling and lead senses into another state, which resembles states that are diagnosed in cases of mental illnesses.

18.) As a source of energy, the spiritual body uses energy coming from nature and the Sun. It absorbs it automatically, consciously, and thoughtfully.

19.) There are photons, which as a central point of the spiritual body, integrate and govern its functions.

Depending on the level of consciousness, photons may operate fully or may sometimes be blocked.

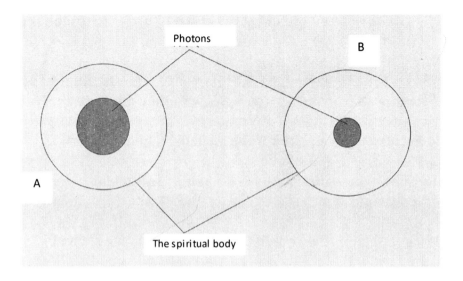

A. The state in which photons operate fully.

B. The state in which photons cannot operate fully, for they are blocked by thoughts of a low frequency.

Fig. 2-2

2. ABOUT THE ORIGIN OF THE WORLD OF SPIRITS AND FACTORS DIVIDING IT

1.) The world of spirits originated due to the group energy of the consciousness of spirits existing as spiritual bodies.

The matter from which our world, as well as our bodies, is made acts in the similar frequency of similar length of waves, which can touch each other and acknowledge their hardness. Matter that is close to the spiritual body of high frequency will be seen and touched by the spiritual body, so it can be used as a building material for forming various worlds and environments.

2.) At different levels of consciousness and frequencies, an infinite number of worlds can be created.

If the frequency of a world is higher, its environment is more harmonic, beautiful, and soothing for the heart. The world of spirits exists, overlapping our own or neighbouring worlds with it, and above every state on the Earth, there are worlds in the layers of different levels of consciousness.

3.) Depending on its form, consciousness may turn into a good or evil spirit.

4.) Turning into a good or evil spirit does not take place after death, but during the lifetime.

While living in the (material) world, people coexist with various levels of consciousness and frequencies. That is why, not after death, but during the lifetime, they turn into good or evil spirits. Very few people are able to reach the level of consciousness equal to that reached by the Buddha, yet it is untrue that "enlightenment is given after death", as Buddhism and many other common beliefs claim. If "enlightenment" means the state of the spirit without blemish, it is necessary to have a pure soul during the lifetime; no third person can help in this process.

5.) The world of spirits and our (material) world disturb each other.

6.) Especially radiation destruction and radioactive contamination cause harm to the world of spirits, almost making its existence impossible.

7.) Photons (the corpus of the spiritual body), which every spiritual body has, have been defined in holy books of various religions for thousands of years in many ways.

The many names by which they are known include: the real I, the essence of being (Buddhist Tathata), Buddha, the nature of Buddha, the divine element, the source of divinity, Lord (in religion *zen*), Atman (breath in the Upanishads' philosophical treaties), life, and the highest wisdom of God.

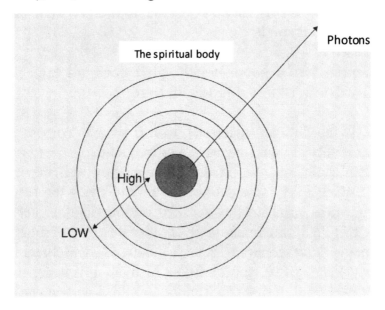

Fig. 2-3

The closer to the centre, the higher the frequency, the shorter the waves, and the higher level of consciousness. We are getting closer to heavenly waves. However, the further from the centre, frequency decreases, waves are longer, and the level of consciousness is lower, as in the case of evil thoughts (Fig. 2-3).

What is plasma, in relation to a proper spirit?

Plasma is an ionised gas, which consists of electrically charged particles that originated due to ionisation. In nature there are many types of plasma, including a solar wind coming from the Sun, the ionosphere surrounding the Earth, or the aurora colouring areas in the polar zone. Plasma is often referred as "the fourth physical state", just after solid, liquid, and gas states. Flames of a fluorescent lamp or gas are types of plasma in our surroundings.

A gas in its usual form plays the role of an isolator, yet in the form of plasma, it is able to conduct electricity, which, while flowing, causes electrons to collide with particles and ions of a gas, producing light characteristic of the gas. It is an electric glow discharge. A composition of a gas mixture influences the type of light and colour of the discharge, just as in the case of the spiritual body, which sends light, changing depending on its internal state.

Plasma differs from an inactive gas in a distinctive way: in plasma, there are Coulomb forces (electric and magnetic forces) between electrically charged particles. In an inactive gas, only a close contact of two particles induces their common reaction, while Coulomb forces have a wider range of operating. That is why a movement of one particle influences many others, inducing various phenomena, which do not take place in the case of an inactive gas.

When Coulomb forces interacting between particles are stronger than its heat energy, plasma goes into a specific state called strongly conjugated plasm, which cannot move so freely. In such situations, its density exceeds a stable level, and complex interactions of Coulomb forces cause the plasma to turn into a set of electrically charged particles, which act like fluid or solid (also Coulomb crystals). This has been tested easily in laboratory conditions.

The spiritual body may also be turned into a solid by regulation of frequency and using properties characteristic of plasma. As we have already seen, plasma includes many free electrons, which make it a good conductor. It must be emphasized that when a current flows through it, an electric field is formed in the nearest area, and this field both influences the acting of the plasma and facilitates moving groups of particles in its interior. This organic integrity (self-organising) has been confirmed by observation. As a result of these properties of plasma, its electromagnetic copy is born and thus, the spiritual body, being plasma, formed and kept self-organising functions such as memory, character, thinking, and consciousness.

Here are summarised the properties of the spiritual body:

— In the centre of the spiritual body there are photons of the highest frequency, which fulfil the main functions.

— The spiritual body is a plasmatic body, consisting of countless electrons and ions, which organically self-organise and keep memory, consciousness, character, and thinking shaped during the lifetime.

— As a result of Coulomb interactions between particles, the spiritual body has the structure of an outer layer with very strong coupling properties.

— Differences of a consciousness level cause changes in the internal state of plasma, which takes various colours and can change its structure and functions, which correspond with a gas, liquid, or solid.

— The spiritual body is a living body, which can take up many forms of a variable structure, from the human body to a spherical body.

Chapter III
Functions of the real I (photons)

Let us now consider the activity of photons, which may be defined as the source of light of the soul, and which we will call "real I" as a tribute to an ancient wisdom. This chapter is an essential part of the book, for it explains the essence of the issues discussed.

Alive or dead, we cannot stop being ourselves. During our lifetimes, consciousness is our companion, and every day seems to be an endless sequence of fights with adversities. Sometimes our world starts to resemble a prison; at other time, we consider it a cosy home that soothes our hearts. We are sculptures of our own psyche, a work of art.

The real I is a command tower that directs the psyche towards harmony, perfection, and creating a higher form of itself. If consciousness is consistent with this direction, it is possible to experience a strong feeling of dominating unity, joy, and calmness, and an undisturbed mind. Acting in this way, the real I leads us towards consciousness, which is hidden in all of us.

Properties of the real I, in different religious, philosophical, and physical systems, have been referred to as:

Pure Energy

Innocent Heart

Creative Force

Overwhelming Ego

Infinite Wisdom

Real I

Unconditional Light

Life Energy

Some more religious names include:

Unity

Divine Element, Source of Divinity

Essence of Being, Real I

Lord (in Zen religion)

Buddha, Nature of Buddha

Atman (breath in the Upanishads' philosophical treaties)

Not-I (Anatman), Highest Soul (Paramatma)

Highest Wisdom of God

This phenomenon cannot be seen by those living without consciousness and aim in life, but only by those engaged in searching the right way and by trying to live in harmony with each other, which earlier was defined by the greatest ones, who were owners of truly living souls.

Especially in the field of religion, the birth of the real I is explained with a type of cosmic activity, which is defined in various ways, such as:

Spirit of Universe

God the Father (Christianity)

Life Energy

Buddha Vairocana (Hinduism)

Creator

Dainichi Nyorai (esoteric Buddhism)

Brahman (breath in the Upanishads' philosophical treaties)

Amitabha (Buddha of Infinite Light, Buddhism of the Pure Land, etc.)

Allah (Islam)

Amenominakanushi (Lord of the holy centre of heaven in the shintō-Japanese religion)

Space Consciousness

Universal Force

God

Consciousness of Life

Idea or Ideal (Plato)

Despite differences in these definitions, we can presume that they define the same thing.

When a thought and consciousness are opposed, or are in conflict with properties of the real I, it causes the following states: distorted thoughts; discomfort or hatred; feelings of alienation or loneliness; arrogance, vanity, or jealousy; conflict, confrontation, or discrimination; depression, feeling of emptiness, despair; "hurt spirit of rivalry"; falling down, decadence, degeneration.

There is nothing more dignified and more worthy of trust than the properly guided human heart, yet there is also no worse ending than that of the same heart when pushed in the wrong direction.

In the previous chapter, I have written that all people own photons and the real I, and their acting may be used completely by some, while others may have these elements weakened due to evil thoughts. Despite these differences, it is crucial to understand that everyone has the real I, this vessel of divine wisdom and the source of light of the soul.

In Buddhism there is a doctrine called *Nyoraizō shisō* (*Tathagatagarbha*) which states that everyone "inside his heart keeps the seed of Buddha (*Nyorai*)". In Persia, the first patriarch of *zen* religion, Bodhidharma, for nine years had been performing *zazen*—a meditation practice, sitting facing the wall—when he finally discovered that all people have hearts as pure as that of Buddha.

Dōgen Kigen, a Japanese *zen Sōtō* Buddhism master, wrote: "We all have internally the nature of Buddha and we cannot deny it, and when we practice, surely we will become enlightened."

Saichō, the founder of the *Tendai* school of Buddhism, was a follower of "one-vehicle" (the theory of the absolute vehicle or system, which collects all humanity towards Enlightenment), which states that we all have an element of Buddha and gain Enlightenment. The victory of Saichō in a dispute with a Tokuichi master, the follower of the *Hosso* school of Buddhism, who was preaching "three-vehicles", is immortalized in historical records. In a great simplification, "three-vehicles" negates the fact of having all natures of Buddha internally.

In the heart of every man, the divine element is present by the nature of the real I, which was explained from the scientific viewpoint in the previous chapter. Concentrating at the real I, all people should understand that they are proud creatures, and if they respect each other as units and stop entering each other's way, they will obtain a shining body. Many people hide in their heads a gold and beautiful light point, which, with spiritual progress, will transform into a resplendent, wider sphere of light. This light is in the place of the third eye, and from an anatomical point of view, it overlaps the pineal gland and pituitary gland, placing it directly in the same place as the centre of the spiritual body; it is photons.

Everyone is a luminous body, which follows one way to spiritual development, to be able to discover completely his divine element and shine with the power of the Sun. This is the truth about man that contemporary Earth-dwellers lost sight of for a long time.

The real I emphasizes that a person needs to develop continually and create a better person. Whenever you go, the real I will follow you. It will appear everywhere and does not let you go away. It will emerge from every direction and force confrontation with a real state of affairs, with reality. The real I does not know mercy and will not leave you alone. It is being and acting, which cannot be avoided by anyone. It can be seen as the source of light for the soul, a command tower and a compass and a radar at the same time.

By the acting of the real I, man gains and consolidates a desire to reach the highest level, in spite of the fact that this desire is already deep-rooted in his heart. Although man stays in a prison of conventions, there is no worry that he will lose entirely his natural dream about life consistent with his own divine element. Impulses, desires, and dynamics, which are hidden in the real I and in the divine element, are able to move even those who are in the chains of conventions and everyday habits. Everyone will follow the real I and will create themselves.

This may not take the form of a conscious creation, but entails discovering and looking for oneself. By selecting thoughts, words, and deeds, it is necessary to erect a bridge connecting us with the acting of the real I and with the source of the divine element, to finally allow them to pass through us. However, daily discipline is necessary to achieve this state. This discipline is discussed in detail in chapter XIV.

The real I hides a psychical depth and consists of many layers, or faces, and discovering them will allow us to become, undoubtedly, united with the source of the divine element. Surely, the main goal of the real I (the soul) is progress. This is the only goal the soul wants to achieve.

The soul desires evolution that is consistent with clear principles. If it makes a mistake or loses its way, it will insistently return on the way of evolution.

Connecting with consciousness of the real I allows us to obtain new understanding and fresh look. Since ancient times, this has been called "enlightenment". A feeling of union with other living creatures and spiritual understanding can be born due to this phenomenon, and noble feelings originate in the heart—feelings such as calmness, joy, and love. In such a moment, frequency of our waves reaches the highest level.

The state at which life reaches the highest frequency is joy in itself. According to Sigmund Freud, the psyche is not a collection of waste products swept to the subconscious, such as contradictions, libido, or expelled matters. It is necessary to understand and believe that we follow the divine element that is hidden in our interior, and finally to start taking care of ourselves. Man is not a sinful creature burdened with original sin, does not have to live in compliance with undecided faith or karma imposed on it, and does not have to ask God for forgiveness.

We must find our value first to be entitled to judge others. Expressing it in Christian terminology, only when we can bless ourselves can we bless the other man. Only when we discover that we are saintly creatures will we be able to see sanctity in others, and it cannot take place in the reverse direction. When we can see only somebody else's value, not knowing our own, we start criticise and hate others, trying to make them equal to us. That is why it is important to understand ourselves properly, to acknowledge our own value and go forward slowly, with little steps in this creative direction.

We all hide an element of sanctity in us. When we deny the fact that we are all the same saintly creatures and allow the state where conflicts and fights appear, the real I will not aim to change the individual, but will direct us to the cause of the conflict. Next, giving the impulse for changes of our understanding and individual lives, it will lead us to the light of the internal divinity and consciousness, which embodies the true I. This activity will result in an impulse coming from our interior, which will mobilise us and never leave us. Even people focused on material benefits and dominated by everyday routine sooner or later will desire to change. These changes will occur when we experience extraordinary abilities, love, empathy, and feelings of unity, openness, understanding, and creativity of the real I in our own bodies.

Chapter IV

Waves of the Soul, the World of Spirits, and its Class Society

1. What are Waves of the Soul?

Even at this moment, from the centre of our being, we are sending energy in all directions. These waves of energy have thoughts, information, and frequency. Your thoughts and deeds turn into energy of vibrations of various colours, which influence surroundings and form the environment proper for the energy. Depending on the soul and consciousness, waves vary, flowing both from the outside and to the inside of our I.

Human thoughts have different lengths of waves, and like words, which are transmitted in the form of a voice by sound waves, consciousness, thoughts, and prayers are transmitted as the energy of consciousness by brain waves. This means that waves of the soul exist. Thoughts of a man pass to three thousand worlds, and this is how they draw things and events.

Equals look for equals. Thoughts and consciousness act like magnets that attract certain consequences. They are like a mother who gives birth to life, for they have power that concentrates around it similar types of energy. They not only make their ideas and wishes real, but also have the power to attract everything that we are afraid of or that arouses fear. Almost all events, circumstances, and environments are products of our consciousness. Each one has an enormous power.

Individual events and adventures are caused by us, so we can create and experience our own real I. The further our thoughts and consciousness go beyond the human level and turn into waves of harmonised thoughts, the more their vibrations become sensitive (frequency increases), their waves become shorter, and finally they reach to the perfect waves from heaven. When egotism and whims cause a lack of harmony, vibrations increase (frequency decreases), waves become longer, and they adjust to those coming from hell, from the underground world.

2. THE WORLD OF SPIRITS AND THE CLASS STRUCTURE OF ITS SOCIETY

Waves from hell mean a state of regress and downfall caused by a self-preserving instinct closed in a thick layer, overgrown ego, and self-defence. We can define them as thoughts full of contradictions, breaches, hostility, and a desire to fight.

In contrast, heavenly waves mean a state when it is possible to show fully the acting of the primary form of the real I and keep our own spirit and body in good health, yet not wanting anything more. With such an attitude, most self-admiration sublimes and turns into care, honesty, and love directed at neighbours, forming a state of harmony and pureness of the soul, which can be defined as the feeling of union of everything (Fig. 4-1).

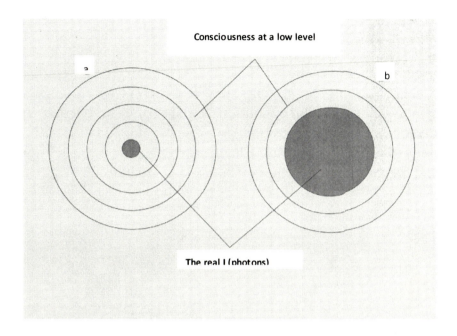

Fig. 4-1. The world of spirits (a kind of class society, which is divided according to waves)

The direction of a healthy evolution of the human psyche is determined. The level of using one's own or someone else's potential, as well as power, beauty, and pureness of psyche and effort for its perfection, are standards for evaluating whether evolution proceeds correctly.

Unless we live in this world, our everyday reality is frequently full of turmoil of the soul, for we fight and worry, staying in the claws of financial problems, or we allow fear, ambitions, or lust to direct us. It is a matter of fact that life as such has great meaning. However, we must not forget that social position, wealth, and approval are criteria of value important only in this world, while in the world of spirits, they are useless. Value estimation criteria which function in our world do not have any justification in the world of spirits. Destination is determined only on the basis of waves of the soul (Fig. 4-2).

We can speak not only about evolution in a strict biological sense, but also about the evolution of matter and psyche. In the former meaning, losing the way of development means gradual psychical falling down, retraction, and regress. The psyche is also forced to develop continuously and evolve, or, in contrast, to retract. Even if it seems that progress has stopped for a while, in fact it means only that we have entered a time of incubation and preparation for further evolution and creation.

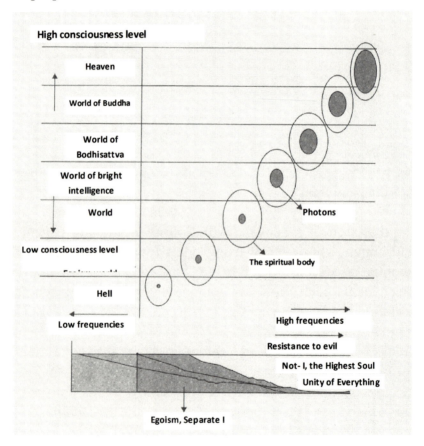

The fact that particular spherical bodies include three levels results from frequency of consciousness extending to these worlds and is caused by some fluctuation of the level of vibrations. For example, due to changing of frequency, the spirit from the World of bright intelligence rises to the

Bodhisattva's world or lowers to the world of good people, yet because keeping high frequency for a long time is particularly difficult, this spirit quite quickly returns at his primary level. Each of the worlds is divided into many layers, so there is an infinitive number of them.

Fig. 4-2 The world of spirits (a kind of class society, which is divided according to waves)

Spiritual evolution, which concerns consciousness, has been forgotten so far and pushed aside by our so prosaic, human, everyday life. Reality concentrates at material and earthly things, treating affairs of the saintly world as ordinary daydreams. The answer to question of what is the evolution and development of consciousness, which from the very beginning should be the commonly accepted basis of existence, has been despised, treated with superiority, and neglected.

The truth of the soul, which says that every man has the brilliant real I and that everyone is a being who is able to plan his conscious spiritual development, for a long time has been forgotten. This has enabled many insidious ideologies and factors, which led humanity to fall down and lose itself in hedonism, to spread. The important truth was lost, and people guided by material wishes started to estimate everything according to the measurement of who is right to exist in this world.

The real I will never stop its pressure, so psychical development leads us or turns us on the way back to create our own ego.

The higher the level of consciousness, the deeper the levels of our being that can be comprehended by us. We extend the scope of ego consciousness and its definition, while people connected with us, events, and our surroundings are perceived by us as continuation of ourselves. At some level of psychic development, we will have to pay attention to everything—what was neglected, ignored, hated, discriminated against or omitted, everything that was forgotten—and then we can face it to finally unite with it.

At the same time, we will be able to comprehend completely all aspects of our being. Development means learning all parts and layers of our I, and deeply understanding them. The direction of healthy evolution of the psyche assumes perfection of the soul, giving up egoism, consistent training of the mind, experiencing the difficulties of this world, and finally the whole development process that allows us to gain the wealth of a strong and pure soul.

Worlds of spirits overlap or neighbour with our world, forming above every state. They also mirror with their colours the history, culture, customs, religion, and consciousness level of particular states. Hierarchically diverse in frequency, the worlds of spirits were not formed by some god or celestial forces, yet like our world, where a great diversity of reality, environments, groups, and cultures exists, heaven and hell originated due to the group energy of consciousness of souls, which is born after death.

The consciousness of an individual and group consciousness create various worlds. This can also be applied to our world and fields such as law, politics, business, architecture, transport, media, and scientific civilisation, whose elements are born in the consciousness and human thoughts simply reflecting them. No one could unite the whole world or take it over, and that is why at the level of the world of spirits it is impossible to understand completely and be aware of the actions of all important persons, activities of organisations and groups, and all changes in the environment. These changes take place under the influence of problems of scientific civilisation and it is impossible to keep continuously alert in relation to them and supervise or keeping conductivity or readiness for instant communication. Absolute confidence is possible as a concept and metaphysical notion; it does not occur in the real world nor in the spiritual world.

In the following subchapters I am going to explain the features and the particular classes of the spiritual world, using Buddhist terminology (ten spiritual kingdoms in Tendai Buddhism).

3. EGOISM WORLD

The egoism world is a place, which is not governed by any law except the law of planning profit and where spirits live concentrating on everyday reality and obsessed with thoughts about their material business. The only subject they consider is their life and surrounding world; they are able to accept only such elements that can be judged with their own measure. The first place is taken by profit and pride, and even if opinion of third persons is correct, they are not able to understand this, for they judge only from their own point of view. Of course they believe that their opinion is the only rightful one.

Egoism of spirits living in this world is tightly connected with consciousness at the low level, and they block themselves and lock themselves within their own limitations. Such spirits expect to be understood, and to lead lives whose conditions are very gentle. They do not have any precise criteria for telling good from evil, which means that their feelings of guilt are not deep and they have no chance of knowing what a harsh judgement is. Even if they receive love, they are not able to comprehend its value, which means that they go through life like blind men. They tie their bodies with ropes of lust and self-affection of their own free will.

In the Egoism world, spirits are slaves of money, religion, egoism, and themselves. They move in groups, whispering in their ears sweet words and accepting without hesitation their hurt personalities and distortions, and their thoughts remain evil, insidious, and sick. These spirits pull like magnet all social problems. They are guilty of all seven cardinal sins defined by the Roman Catholic Church: wrath, greed, sloth, pride, lust, envy, and gluttony. They like silly jokes and they are glad, when influenced by caprice, that they can hurt someone. They can feel various evil emotions, which are obstacles for their development, and even if they are aware of the fact that they cannot go on in this way, they are not able to change their lifestyles or consciousness and find a new look at their existence, so finally they return to the starting point. It is difficult to go up, because everything is measured by their very low own I.

4. THE WORLD OF GOOD PEOPLE

This world, so different from the one described above, is inhabited by spirits whose egoism is far weaker, and who are spirits of a good nature. However, they can be attracted only by the privileges, social status, and money of this world, and at the same time, they support it. It is difficult for them to look at their own position, for they are united with these attributes, live in a castle full of artificial splendour, holding in their hearts vanity, arrogance, and the assumption of their own wisdom. Dwellers of this world are interested in the opinions of others about them, and such opinions influence their self-assessment, which is the basis for everything in their usual life. The ego of the spirits, which are under the influence of material things, adorning themselves with various spangles and careful that no one can even touch them, grows, having for food the firm spirit of competition and vanity (overgrowth of the ego).

The dwellers of the world of good people are too attached to everything worldly. They are not rotten to such a degree that they do evil deeds voluntarily, yet their progress is not sufficient enough to do good. And in spite of the fact that they are hurt by biases and seeing the world through earthly eyes, they have stopped at a not-so-high mental level, and their intellectual training is not sufficient. They come from behind due to their emotional development. Feelings of gratefulness and devotion usually mean that we think and treat others just like ourselves. However, very often such behaviours appear only in situations when we can use them to our own advantage.

5. THE WORLD OF BRIGHT INTELLIGENCE

In the world of bright intelligence, there are spirits that are artistically and scientifically gifted. They are remarkable in particular fields of science and art, yet it makes them self-important. That is why this level assembles spirits of horizons which are limited by their own narrow circle of interests. And since this is a dominant tendency, this world spreads from the level inhabited by spirits dealing with issues of domination, selection, and competitiveness, as well as paying attention to ambitions, privileges, and social position, up to higher levels, where only noble feelings can be found.

Among scientists, cases of egocentrism that accompanying weak emotional development are not rare, and a great mind is only sometimes bounded by social adjustment. In this group, compulsive and perfectionist dispositions are very strong, usually leading to obsession, and in many cases, this is connected to problems related to human relations. Spirits of well-developed minds and a strong desire to obtain power, combined with obsessiveness and low morals, may turn into leaders of evil spirits, who will dare to challenge the will of heaven.

Dwellers of this world usually separate themselves from others with a distinct line. It is certain that they are not ready to sacrifice for their neighbours; even if they do what they can, they will not try to move a single step more. In many cases, ordinary spirits who live in the previously described world of good people obtain deeper truth and wisdom, for they have been shaped by every day and life experiences, in contrary to the spirits from the world of bright intelligence.

Only in the higher spheres of the world described in this point can we find more spirits who, because of their scientific research, contribute to the development of the world and have humble and honest characters. There are also spirits who find deeper emotions and serve others, giving them joy and vitality through artistic expression.

6. THE WORLD OF BODHISATTVA

Dwellers of the World of Bodhisattva keep their bodies and spirits in good health. However they are not interested in and do not worry about themselves more than is necessary, sacrificing themselves for others, which is a very natural way for them. This is a world of spirits where it is easy to manifest feelings of a higher level, which are characterised by taking care of neighbours and the readiness to sacrifice oneself. A barrier separating their egos from other spirits is very thin. They are very kind and find joy in serving others. They are able to rise above an apparent value and subjective feelings to leave in the first place all deeds indicated by the senses. They do not forget that they live and work to serve others, and they discover in themselves wisdom, which makes them able to judge whether they can use fully their potential for their own life, work, and human relations.

Unfortunately, their minds have not reached greater depth and complexity. They want to dress up and are eager for praise by others. As opposed to dwellers of the world of Buddha, who fulfil their duties given by a certain mission, spirits from the world of Bodhisattva perform not what they have to, but what they are able to do, for they have a more developed consciousness, which in a natural way puts others in first place. They are very useful for the world and society.

7. THE WORLD OF BUDDHA

This world is a place whose dwellers have chosen as their mission a fight with evil living in society and in human souls. In this place, both their own desires and potential are not valued, and the main criterion of activities is the mission to be accomplished. That is why creatures inhabiting this world are called angels.

Their mission requires them to be resistant to evil and to be able to detect it, and also requires intuition and the skill of prediction. When their talent and soul are of a great value, the mission to fight with evil makes them lead extraordinary lives. They must learn a lot, for their faith is very harsh and hard. For sure, a peaceful and calm life is not their role.

The mission may mean freeing people from wrong thinking or prejudice. Another time they will correct psyches and arouse conscience, or encourage, which is very important when changing systems that are dysfunctional. Usually this meets with hostile reactions, for their mission reveals everything that is hidden in the shadow sphere of the soul. That is why, while completing their mission, they are very careful not to flaunt their deeds that are performed correctly; they stay "behind the curtains". While in the shadow, they give support, lead to the right way, carefully observe the course of events, rectify shortages, and prepare everything in such a way that people are able to follow in the direction of development completely unaided.

Dwellers in the world of Buddha are experts in various fields and owners of a well-developed intellect, deeply understanding and experiencing the feelings of unity of everything. They fulfil their faith as those who bring light and truth to the world. Since they act on the basis of predicted future, they can become the type of light that is able to wake people up, and their characters are so pure that we can almost feel their saint element.

Sometimes it happens that as symbols of free travelling through all levels and worlds, they wear wings, which during fight can turn into a shield. When they feel that it is necessary, they can open for man the way of spirits and transfer all necessary information. Since the dawn of man, angels, heavenly knights have been fighting with the devil, who symbolises the victory of evil, for the soul of man. Fulfilling the role of apostles, heavenly messengers, and performers of divine orders, angels never stop performing supervision and directing work of especially important people, organisations, and groups of people.

8. Heaven

There has not any notion that has frightened people more or brought them greater peace and more terrible torments, than the word "God". It is obvious, that, as Einstein said, God in the human form, the almighty Creator of Heaven and Earth, cannot exist. Yet if we understand "God" to mean 'energy of life", "power of creation", or "universal power of the universe, which pushes it to development", we can use such notion.

In times of ignorance and superstition, all saint spirits were perceived as gods. Saint spirits mean souls of great people, who were born according to evolution laws and created a great circle of life. They would not be able to humiliate heaven, nor to despise it. Perceived as gods, in fact, archangels are humans from beyond the Earth, who came from far away around 12 thousand years ago. This fact is not known to modern terrestrials.

Even those who are defined as gods from the heavens used to live as human beings. And as humans just like us, many times they experienced sadness or tragedies. They had, obviously, their own faults, yet due to hard training and the perfection of their soul, they gained personality and consciousness that allowed others to worship them as gods.

They were born and educated in a civilisation that overtook not only the earthly civilisation in the times when they arrived on our planet, but even the modern one, so it is no wonder that, as creatures of highly developed consciousness, they were gods to terrestrials. And those wonderful persons were being subjected to various trials and hardened as heavenly messengers, but a long-standing self-perfection gave them the ability to undertake right decisions. Otherwise they would not be able to see through the devious methods of evil spirits or hypocrites preaching justice and love, just as they would not be able to understand human feelings, nor lead this world on the right way.

Saint spirits from heaven are wise men and masters filled with grace and love, on whom you can depend, for they have wider life experience than we do. It is not surprising that they are respected and admired, yet it is necessary to know that it is a serious mistake to treat them as objects of cult or idolatry.

They come from the same source, and include persons from the world of religion who left a lot of serious studies. According to the heavenly plan, in every time a prophet or saint who fit his times was revealed. For example, when people started losing hope and common sense because of successive calamities, including raging epidemic or poverty, when deceitful thoughts and deeds were spreading or when misinterpretations of holy books were being propagated, there was always someone who brought hope and relief to people, giving them clues adjusted to their level of knowledge and maturity.

Religion for two thousand years has been a religion explained in accordance with the climate, life rules, consciousness, and level of knowledge that functioned two thousand years ago. When one epoch passes, its tastes, thoughts, and words undergo changes, as do its people's chiaroscuro, textures, and colours. That is why we need to understand history from two thousand or four thousand years ago to feel and understand the knowledge and atmosphere that were crucial elements for people of that time. We will not be able to comprehend in any other way that the lessons provided and taught by religion mirror methods adapted to a particular epoch and the level of consciousness functioning at that time.

At the top of the heavenly hierarchy, there is a creature, which is called by various names, including Jehovah, Yahweh, Allah, and God Father, but all these refer to the same person, and it is the soul of a man who reached spiritual heights, and seven archangels fulfil the roles of his supporters and can be found in the Apocrypha of the Old and New Testaments—Michael, Gabriel, Raphael, Uriel, Sariel, Teliel, and Usiel.

At the beginning, during the assembling of works that would become the New Testament, over eighty gospels, which allegedly described Jesus' words and deeds, existed, but only four were chosen. They are the gospels of Matthew, Marc, Luke, and John. These gospels were written in Greek after Jesus' death, in the second half of the first century. It means, that at the beginning of Christianity, there was a large group of writings called Apocrypha, which were not included to the Bible. However, it was very natural that the process of deification of Jesus took place, for this is how the Church could keep its power and raise its authority, and the choice of writings was easy to spread among the Romans.

It is a matter of fact that at the dawn of Christianity, there were many books, which carried various thoughts.

Let us look at the example of the most important of the seven archangels, whose name appears both in the Old and in the New Testament. In the Muslim Koran, he is presented as Mikail, who announces revelations with Jibra'il, or Gabriel. Young Joan of Arc was given a mission and led towards it by Michael. Even before Jesus' birth, Michael appears to Mary with archangel Gabriel to announce the Good News. When a missionary, Franciszek Ksawery, came to Japan, he proclaimed that the islands were subject to the archangel Michael; even today, he is a guardian angel of that country.

What about archangel Gabriel?

— For around twenty years, he announced revelations to Mahomet.

— He announced to the Blessed Virgin Mary the birth of Jesus.

—He announced to Elisabeth, Zachariah's wife, that she would give birth to John the Baptist. It was also he who announced to Joseph, while he was sleeping, the blessed state of the Blessed Virgin Mary.

—He took part in the baptism of Jesus Christ.

So his name appears not only in the Old and New Testaments, but also in the Koran.

In Biblical times, creatures from heaven were concentrated in relation to the Hebrew nation, particularly to Abraham, pointing the only right way and morality, which marked the beginning of serious engagement of heavenly creatures in human affairs.

In later times, in every epoch, these creatures incarnated in people representing various nations and states, raising their consciousness and teaching, and finally leading their times in fields of study, art, culture, law, politics, and religion. They were giving enlightenment, eradicating prejudices and illusions from the past. They contributed a lot to humanity, raising their level of consciousness with progress and development in various fields.

In modern times, the state of science on Earth has developed considerably, despite losing balance with the spiritual, which has caused some problems, and there are more people who are able to judge in a scientific and rational way. After all, the attempt to launch a flying object into space was successful. Also such great prophets as Buddha, Abraham, John, Jesus Christ, Moses and Muhammad are exceptional souls who were incarnated by saint spirits from heaven.

Chapter V

Incarnation and incarnated spirits

I should write some words of explanation on the subject of incarnation and incarnated spirits.

The history of the soul begins with the moment of zygote formation. In the third month after conception, the soul is incarnated by a spirit, whose consciousness is acquired.

The newly formed soul of man is not identical with the incorporated spirit. When a superior creature appeared on the Earth, it was man, and when ten thousand years ago, the frontal lobe was developed, spirits that regarded our planet to be at a satisfying level of evolution decided to settle here and make an attempt to incarnate into people directly, to raise their consciousness.

They did not limit their activities to extending human consciousness. It was they who planned the evolution of our psyche by causing it to experience misery, happiness, and sadness, and by testing it. By means of telepathy, they discovered for people sources of knowledge and spread seeds of scientific findings, and also encouraged them to take up some fields of art, trying to stimulate in this way development of all civilisations.

The notion of "previous incarnations" refers to a spirit's life, which incarnates, yet a newly formed soul in which the spirit has incarnated does not have any previous incarnations. And the new soul is under the influence of consciousness of the incarnated spirit. Its character becomes similar, just like its way of thinking, interests, models of behaviour, profession, etc. In other words, it takes the form that is a modern counterpart of other human beings who lived in the past.

Therefore, their faults are also the same. That is why, we should not be surprised that works written by incarnated spirit in the past are researched and verified anew in our times by a newly born soul.

Two spirits, spirit and soul, will never be one and they will always be two separate beings. Usually they follow different paths in the moment of death.

Chapter VI
Behaviour models of evil spirits

I must write a few words about evil spirits, who live in the lowest levels of the egoism world, emitting negative thoughts, waves, and energy.

I have already mentioned that there is a fight for human souls between spirits of heaven and evil spirits. The course of this fight of spirits of heaven and evil spirits, who use smart manoeuvres and tricks with great skill, influences the spreading of healthy thoughts, ways of life, and relations between people, or makes tricky and vicious ideas and ways of life the main stream.

Human weakness, lust, ignorance, lack of knowledge, and insufficient objection against evil may be considered the source of the power of evil spirits.

A decent man may believe that after his death, he will be welcomed and blessed by friends, relatives, and saint spirits in the spiritual world, whereas evil spirits will not be welcomed by anyone and will be pulled into a circle of evil very similar to them, or they will be used by evil as messengers. Such a spirit will be left for a very long time alone, unless he sees his mistakes. He will become a dweller of a gloomy world, created by his own consciousness. It is important to know that spirits do not become evil after death; the metamorphosis takes place during their lifetime.

Wallowing in filthy and shady habits, evil spirits take various forms and put on masks only to deceive people, yet their wretched characters finally reveal them. They laugh whenever someone is depraved and loses his right way, and they are glad to see the process of falling down. Because they have never shared any happy or blissful moments with good spirits, they interrupt people in their way to happiness and make plots so people can experience unhappiness, suffering, humiliation, and sadness, which are ordinary elements of their existence.

Sometimes it happens that evil spirits possess people walking through life in a hedonistic way and appreciating only the present moment and use them as messengers of evil, so that they spread unhappiness in the world, or the spirits manipulate them so smartly that these people are convinced that they do good.

Evil spirits also use false miracles, unnatural phenomena, and methods of spiritual development. So, among miracles and parapsychological abilities, which seem to come from heaven, there are some that are works of evil spirits. At the beginning they support spiritual leaders and people being mediums, saying that all they need to do good is consciousness and then they demand payment and use their followers, making them jointly responsible for spreading evil and pulling them to the ranks of evil. At the beginning they guess what bothers their followers, bringing them temporary joy, but finally accuse them of lack of faith or contributions that are too small and deprive them of everything. They use the same methods as villains of this world. Because of their manipulation, their followers, unconsciously, become a part of the circle of evil spirits.

Evil spirits desire to be worshipped and treated like saviours and receive oblations of money. They prey on the souls of pious people, copying saint spirits in sending revelations. Beware of those especially who are members of religious organisations or depend on people with parapsychological abilities.

Evil spirits usually prey on sensitive people, who can be easily directed, depriving them of the ability to make correct judgements; many times they push them into traps and finally overtake them. Sometimes, they create optical illusions, just as when someone uses a projector, or they evoke some images in people's heads, acting on the retina. It is very difficult to see the differences in perception of the environment caused by a sort of autohypnosis of auditory hallucinations, auto-suggestion, dreams, or desires, yet we will be able to judge it on our own, if we do it in the wider context and make use of our common sense.

Evil spirits possess people who are filled with feelings related to jealousy, envy, hatred, wrath, or grief and create in them the need to cleanse through easing these emotions.

Amazingly intelligent, yet at the same time emotionally immature, the leader of evil does not trust people. He is a loner-perfectionist who is tormented with obsessions and who entirely despises people. Believing in his own elitism and desiring to make all of humanity his slaves, he uses various metaphysical ideas and ideologies (Nazism, communism, or terrorism, for example) in trying to subjugate people. His intelligence does not go hand-in-hand with character, morality, or mature emotions, and his genius used for evil purposes often leads to tragedy.

Evil spirits use ideologies and ideas to direct people, yet they do not believe in these metaphysical conceptions. Instead, they laugh at them and despise those who trust them. It needs to be mentioned here that people who identify themselves with fundamentalist ideas and ideologies became very similar to evil spirits a long time ago, and now they are observed and mocked by those spirits.

Sometimes it happens that evil spirits tell the truth. They lead people in the wrong direction in such a way that the directed people are not aware of it. They incarnate themselves into victims, put rotten apples into the holy books, and confront religions. They try to incite humans of various creeds, intellectually and ideologically, provoking fights in this way. People of deep faith are led in the name of God by evil spirits, who distort the messages of religious leaders and then take power over the faithful, by causing them to quarrel with one another.

While directing all these conflicts, evil spirits never reveal their true faces. As a result, human history has always been marked with the blood and tears of religious and ethnic wars.

If we want to make a man his own puppet, according to the methods used by evil spirits, we must sow fear in him and create the belief that we are the only chosen ones and others are bad. Next we need to confirm to him that only our sect or religion is the right one, and finally we must make him a slave of our conception. Offering all the mystical sensations and breathtaking feasts and celebrations for the divine majesty, we must deceive those who will be enthralled with our efforts. Everything will remain a deception, which has nothing to do with the primary faith.

Hostile behaviour directed against the community of a religious sect is called *"hōnan"* (repressions). This is a method according to which all followers are accused of having too little faith and making monetary contributions that are too low. They are threatened with misfortune and illness, and fear is inserted into their hearts. These methods are used even by the Buddhist community, which also has been infiltrated by these spirits. To sum up, in this world, good and evil spirits cross paths trying to influence human consciousness and senses, and also freely enter and live in our bodies.

Chapter VII
Possession

Possession is a state in which the spirit of a particular person is completely controlled by a spirit of evil, and it is usually mistaken for some sort of mental disorder, such as a split personality, epilepsy, or a mental illness. There are so many incidents caused by possession that they cannot be taken lightly. Apart from existing in the visible world, there are many others instances in which spirits interact with people.

Many spirits, in place of going to hell, wander in our world. When we start thinking about something with a negative attitude, an evil spirit may use this frequency and possess us. If you try to help a lost spirit, he will use it and possess you, for he wants only to help himself.

Matters of the spirits are settled at the level of the world of spirits; is better for us not to interfere.

Spirits of the dead, animals, and vindictive spirits of a low level of consciousness despise and possess all those people who pay attention to earthly judgement criteria and are subject to the desires and lusts of this world. These spirits multiply befouled places on the Earth in place of creating new saint regions. Such spirits possess people who are controlled by the idea of finding pleasure, and then they poison the souls of these, people pushing them to do evil in the world.

Unfortunately, sometimes even people who are aware of existing evil spirits are deceived by their tricks and fulfil their every order, losing the way set out by heaven and allowing themselves to be manipulated. These are the circumstances of possession.

Chapter VIII

Guarding spirits and guiding spirits

Guarding spirits and guiding spirits are entirely different from evil spirits who possess people.

Strong bonds connect guarding spirits to us, forming a relationship between the souls reminiscent of the relationship between siblings or that of a student with a master. They are present on our side by order of heaven and they are creatures that guard us, worry about us, lead us, watch us, and give us love. They protect us against the influence of evil spirits, which deceive us and deter us from striving and attempting to get up and try again when we stumble.

A guarding spirit makes contact with a man (through the voice of the heart or telepathy), shares his difficulties, gives courage and clues, and stimulates ambitions. It keeps making attempts to instil in the man a high consciousness and to make his life fruitful. However, man does not pay attention to the spirit's presence, because the fragile waves of the guarding spirit are destroyed by the dilemmas and low, rapid thoughts of the man, which are born during his turbulent lifetime. Sometimes the spirit only watches the man in a difficult situation, for he knows that suffering and trials can develop this human being. If something good happens to us, it is not due only to us. We should be naturally thankful to heaven and the good creatures who protects us on heavenly command.

Guiding spirits are superior spirits, which cooperate with guarding spirits. They role is to help in changing the social role of a man, in accordance with his psychical development, giving particular tips directly relating to his work, giving new missions, or supporting him on his way to scientific discoveries or other endeavours.

CHAPTER IX
PARAPSYCHOLOGY AND PARAPSYCHOLOGICAL ABILITIES

We assume that stimulation of the pineal gland and diencephalon may accelerate development of parapsychological abilities, but there is no direct evidence for it.

There are people in this world—from prophets passing on messages of superior spirits, to ordinary persons described as mediums, and finally to us—who truly are able to communicate with spirits. Both good and evil spirits are able to recognise immediately a man who has such skills. He must be careful to have good thoughts and a pure heart, and he must try to keep himself in the band of high frequencies. Otherwise, he may be used as home for a lost or evil spirit, and as a result, he may be mistakenly diagnosed with a psychical disorder.

The most important—and the most difficult—task is to distinguish good spirits from evil ones. It often happens that an unaware medium allows himself to be manipulated and repeats information that is sent by an evil spirit pretending to be a good one.

A man who is a medium must have an especially pure and good heart, and also should be sufficiently strict with himself and learn how to assess situations correctly, for he is an object of a greater numbers of threats than other people. If he becomes famous both the man and his incarnated spirit become more powerful and more self-confident, and he may develop the incorrect assumption that he is better than others. When money and reputation become too important to a man, evil spirits may gather around him, giving guarding spirits and good spirits very limited access to him. The only thing left is to hope that he will understand everything that is happening around him.

The highest could show the man the way of the spirits within two or three days, yet they do not do it without a serious reason, for it bears a risk. Just as ordinary people can consider reality only according to their own criteria, those who are owners of parapsychological abilities can communicate only with the level of frequency equal to human waves. Unless you are a superior creature from a higher frequency level, you cannot communicate with spirits living there.

The same fate is shared by high-frequency spirits, who cannot communicate with people whose frequency is not high. Even if they succeed, it will not be possible to catch the waves of the spirits, for they are jammed by large vibrations. People who are mediums can see only the part of the spiritual world that is visible from their viewpoint, and this is only a small part of the spirit world. And just as spirits can transmit information that is understood to them and what can be assessed by them, man will read only the information that is compatible with his level of perception and sense. Everyone understands only the world that fits him.

Sometimes it happens that a medium is not aware of his own gift, and potentially, we all have parapsychological abilities. This is no more remarkable than the fact that one person is good at sports and another paints nicely. A medium communicates what has been already said by the spirit standing at a higher level of development than ours, and in other words, is a sort of secretary to him. The majority of such people are able to contact at most the world of egoism and the world of good people; not as many can establish contact with and receive information from the world of Buddha, angels, and heaven.

Supernatural phenomena and parapsychological abilities, which are usually seen in terms of miracles, are not the result of human skill only. They are possible only with contribution of spirits, who simply find scientific use of natural laws, acting on their own or joining their powers in groups.

As I have mentioned previously, the spiritual body in a plasmatic body, and its abilities are limited. That is why a blind faith in spiritual powers, putting high trust in the supernatural powers of the spiritual world, as well as ceremonies, feasts, and faith that propagate such conviction, are characteristic of the limited world of superstitions.

Chapter X

What is the obstacle to correct understanding?

1. Negative results of religions: Islam, Judaism, Christianity, and Buddhism.

The title of this chapter assumes there is a "correct understanding," which means there is a system that enables the functioning and regulation of the process of thinking, methods, consciousness, and society in such way as to most benefit and facilitate human relations.

A lot of people, since they were children, and before they could comprehend anything, had inculcated in them the knowledge whose name is religion, knowledge without any scientific grounds and which is defined as the truth. These people are told that the canon of their religion is the only one, and they are brought up in a culture in which feasts and celebrations connected to particular religious rites are something as natural as the surrounding air. The majority of these people accept religion as a custom. This is repeated by Catholicism, Protestantism, Judaism, Islam, and Buddhism.

It is unthinkable to doubt the presented truth and content of holy books of a particular religion, for they infiltrate deeply and influence the way of thinking of people, their philosophy, law, lifestyles, and value system. This raises many problems even today, in scientifically enlightened times These beliefs are an obstacle to understanding and judging on the basis of common sense.

The harmful activities of many ideologies and dogmas are connected to this issue, as is the whole defence mechanism, which manifests itself in the characteristics of brain functions and psychological processes.

In this chapter we will trace the history of religion and describe its current state, and then we will explore its connections to ideologies, dogmas, characteristics of brain functions, and the whole defence mechanism of a man.

Around four thousand years ago, saint spirits, who came from the same source, started to engage in many places, states, and epochs to solve important problems of old times and pass on, through extraordinary teachers, the will of heaven to people. And though it was difficult to penetrate the customs, intellectual level, and particular features of the times, the saint spirits tried to keep up with those times and give clues to people that were adequate for the development of their knowledge. Later on, they warned about new interpretations and incorrect understanding of prophecies, and tried to explain to people the merit of the right way.

Even with such a wide-ranging point of view, there is no single holy book that explains all truths, and methods and stages of such explanations may vary. However, every holy book includes some truth. Despite the variety of such works, the basic message is the same. Apparent differences were created by human interpretation. Obviously, the holy books of Judaism, Christianity, Islam, and Buddhism are overflowing with truths and important words that constitute the source of light for human souls. These teachings of great souls, whose hearts were devoted and whose lives were risked to spread the message, should receive their due tribute.

In the meanwhile the main problems are distortions, fabrications, and misrepresentations caused by scientists, people of religion, and those who engaged in editing holy books in later times. As a result, a particular problem is an excessive deification of the forefathers of religion, which was started to strengthen a particular church and its community. The teachings of these churches are wrongly spread as words spoken by their creators. The negative consequences are enormous.

The name of God is used as a tool to govern people. Rulers use it indiscriminately to tell others that all wars are waged in the name of God, that all massacres are consistent with His will. Religious ceremonies and feasts glorify sovereigns and add luster to them.

To be sure, no one would like to think that their professed religion is wrong, and probably every believer presumes that his is the only right truth. Man does not live and cannot live doubting what he believes in. For all—religion and state, culture and tradition—support man's identity and awareness of being a part of community.

If such elements heal and become a sort of shelter for the soul, especially in relation to religion, no one would dare to challenge its forms or saint doctrines. In the context of the holy book of every religion, raising doubts is treated as a betrayal, and any attempt to present a new perspective on it is perceived as blasphemy.

For monotheistic religions, believers perceive their agreement with God, and that is why any doubt in His words is equal to apostasy, leading to loss and negation of faith, which imposes a real threat in the form of breaching the agreement. The genealogy of the monotheistic religion of the Semites did not accept any other gods; that is why Jehovah, Yahweh, Allah, and God Father is only one person and only divided between particular religions.

Moses, Jesus Christ, and Muhammad, who received revelations and directions from archangels, with Michael and Gabriel ahead, on command of Jehovah, are also only one person, yet due to many interpretations of people belonging to various creeds, they are presented as Gods of different religions, which must be fought against.

Let us take the point of view of Islam.

In the moment of leaving this world, Muhammad, just like Moses (who was given the Ten Commandments by archangel Gabriel over three thousand years ago), received the Twelve Commandments from archangel Gabriel.

Here are the Twelve Commandments of Muhammad:

1.) You shall love only one God.

2.) Honour and love your father and your mother.

3.) You shall love your neighbour and give what he needs.

4.) You shall defend weaker travellers and foreigners.

5.) You shall not waste anything.

6.) You shall not desire.

7.) You shall not fornicate.

8.) You shall not kill.

9.) You shall not desire property of your neighbour, and in particular property of orphans.

10.) You shall not cheat in trade.

11.) You shall not behave unwisely.

12.) You shall not be haughty.

The following words are found in the Ten Commandments of Moses: "You shall not make idols." Idolatry is also forbidden in Islam. Another command states: "Remember the Sabbath day, to keep it holy," yet for Christianity it is Sunday, for Judaism it is Saturday, and for Islam, Friday. Still, this does not change the meaning of the Ten Commandments and Twelve Commandments.

Among nomads who used to live in inhospitable wilderness, blood relations in particular communities were so strong that leaving a group meant death for an individual. In the past, there were incidents of blending blood between tribes, and on one land there were followers of Judaism and Christianity, so it was necessary to form a system that would make the coexistence of various groups and religions much easier. The metaphysical idea of the almighty, only God, who cannot be seen and touched, was too abstract for the minds of nomadic tribes, especially since each one was devoted to its own god, so they were limited to idolatry, blood connections, and relations with land.

Yet when God and religion transformed into more universal notions, people started liberating themselves from the old value systems.

Muhammad had been preaching a new faith for twenty years, from the time when he was forty-three until his death at sixty-three. Jesus Christ conducted similar activities for only three years, while Buddha did so for as long as forty-five years. The Koran regulates all matters in every detail, including trade transactions; perhaps the fact that Muhammad was a businessman influenced this issue.

Teachings of the Koran concern social life, including marriages, inheritance, trade transactions, sharing one's wealth; matters related to the state, such as the order to preserve justice, common good, criminal law, and the judiciary; and points relating to activities connected with faith and its spiritual aspects. All details are similar to modern law, for they regulate every aspect of life, starting from spiritual life, principles of acting, family life, social rules and ending at religious life. However, in the present age of science, these teachings are gradually departing from reality. Being inviolable, the canon is turning into chains, and this is one of the most crucial reasons for difficulties in the world of Islam.

Let us have a look at other religions.

In contrast to the Koran, which was written by Muhammad with his own hand during the twenty years of his teaching, both the Old Testament from the Moses' times and the New Testament regarding Jesus Christ are texts that were edited several hundred years after the incidents were said to have taken place, and many times some excerpts were deleted and others were introduced. The same took place in the case of Buddhist writings.

The most serious issue separating Judaism, Christianity, and Islam is the issue of prophets and the Messiah. Judaism does not believe that the Messiah has revealed himself, and that is why Jews did not recognise Jesus Christ and crucified him as a false Messiah.

Christianity does not accept Muhammad as a prophet, yet Islam recognises the five great prophets (people who were chosen by God to pass His words): Jesus Christ, Muhammad, Moses, Abraham, and Noah. Islam is right in this issue. According to teachings of Islam, Jesus Christ was one of the great prophets sent by heaven, but he is not the Messiah.

The Messiah (Saviour) is only an abstract, notion, born of optimistic imagination, a person who has never appeared and will never appear. Yet even if the Messiah had come to this world, Jesus Christ showed that if he had started preaching, he would have been criticised, accused, and finally killed.

The Jews were people chosen by heaven. They started with Abraham, the descendant of Sem, who in turn descended from Sumer-Noah, yet incarnated spirits from heaven and guiding spirits also passed information to other prophets: Elias, Jeremiah, and Ezekiel.

In 1250 BC, on Jehovah's command, the archangels Michael and Gabriel passed to Moses a revelation. They directed him and concentrated his activities to serve his people. There is no doubt that by imposing particular life standards on Moses' people, giving them wisdom, harshly punishing them for immoral acts, and educating them, the archangels were striving to make them an example for other nations. It was the first step in positively influencing other people as well.

When the times of the New Testament came, according to the changed will of heaven, the blessing was due for not only one nation, yet for almost all people. However, followers of Judaism, like capricious children, could not relinquish their consciousness of being the chosen nation. That is why they still despise dogmas belonging to other religions, even those that do not mention Jesus Christ or Muhammad.

Meanwhile, Christianity based its whole metaphysical doctrine on a great fiction, in which "the only God is the almighty and omniscient creator of the universe", and in order to keep this belief in the modern world of advanced science, the science must be denied. Such opposition is surprising. Jesus Christ never said that he was the only child of God. There is no doubt that it was fiction produced by scientists and men of religion who wanted to increase the prestige and authority of the Church by deification of Christ, while editing the Bible.

During the editing of the Bible, many forgeries and distortions of the text occurred, and all discrepancies were deleted or burnt. Christianity is not the only religion for which this has happened. A wrong-headed belief, which magnifies the discrepancy with science and preaches a more fundamental and literal understanding of the hold book, is the cause and result of this.

It can be assumed that Islam, which does not have a hierarchical system among clergymen, chose the right form. In Judaism and Christianity, the hierarchical system was always used to condemn everything that could pose a threat to the authority of the clergy, its power, and its wealth. Jesus wore simple clothes and rode on a donkey, while some modern clergy show off in Rolls Royces and dress in rich brocades.

Each religion started from the deification of its founder; later personification and deification of a thought itself took place. The words were written in the form of a holy book, and the accompanying myths forged "reality". New interpretations were born that would surprise even the creators of the religion.

Everything was done to strengthen the clergy's authority. It is not a stretch to state that the clergy have always made the faithful dependent and negated their autonomy. They put forth the concept of original sin and changed their own image while not allowing their followers to change and grow in psychical terms. They have manipulated their followers and allowed them to live in ignorance.

The holy books were written in times when the level of human consciousness was extremely low. Now they are only dead letters that do not jibe with present-day reality, and their words have become a curse. The character of religion, so contradictory to science and closed, has made it lose any power it had to resolve problems of the modern world.

Many faithful, like young children, look for support in the great Messiah or other images of God, finding in them relief and the sense of being safe. This faith in a protecting force, whom we petition for help, does not help in the maturing and development of the man. It does not allow people to make independent judgements and allows fictional metaphysics to manipulate them.

God, the Creator of the universe, is depicted as someone very close to the same level as man. At the same time it is taught: "Be afraid of fiery and revengeful God, be afraid for He shall be your Judge on the Last Day. A dreadful punishment shall be the price for every offence against the God's Law." This simply reflects the intentions of organisations such as the Church. The Church judges and rewards in the name of God, and barbarian acts as genocide have been justified using the holy books.

Mind control, which has been around for four thousand years, instilled fear in man, successfully stopping him from any attempts to doubt and ask questions about new ideas or elements of faith and refusing him the right to return to sources of teaching and listening to the voice of the heart. Despite the fact that man did not commit any crime, he was told, "You will not be saved, for you are weighted with original sin, so pray to your God for forgiveness."

This hurt human dignity and burdened man with feelings of guilt. It gave him a distorted image of himself. Then he was told that only the church could solve his problems and save him.

Certainly, the creation of high culture and paving the way for civilisation and scientific discovery would not have been possible without the image of God causing fear. In times of uncivilised society of a low level of consciousness, inculcation of fear was necessary to teach about morality and ethics. However, this was appropriate only at the primary stage.

The present concept of religion causes dysfunction in society and conflicts that result from the clashing of value systems. Criticism or condemnation of that which is different in other religions was and is used particularly to encourage stronger internal bonding of the community. Exclusion of other religions makes it easier to propagate the idea of a chosen nation or one community teaching about the highest truth. But the image of Christ himself, who preached understanding and unconditional love, is hardly seen. The primary function of religion—the planning and developing of interior and spiritual maturity—has been eliminated.

Ironically, the interior functioning of particular religious sects proceeds without any difficulties, yet when they are confronted with other sects, it causes mutual slandering, attacking, and laughing, leading all the way to killing the opponents.

In every holy book of the three great monotheistic religions, there is a list of commandments and rights given by God to the people. These address various areas of life, such us behaviour, meals, clothes, duties, holidays, and ceremonies. Interpretations of these commandments have caused violent arguments, both outside and inside particular religions, and even Buddhism has not been immune to conflict.

A "message sent from heaven" considers hygienic conditions, examples of behaviour, relations of men and women, conventions, customs related to love and marriages, and style of life, all of which were appropriate for a particular epoch. In the case of Islam, even spiritual aspects of life were regulated in detail. Probably in bloody times, when Islam was born, it was decided without any far-reaching findings, that the Arab world would not function well as one great community.

The Koran, in contrast to the books of other religions, is a direct record made by Muhammad himself, consistent with revelations and so consistent with the will of heaven. Strong opposition against all changes in commandments is natural, but these commandments are far too detailed. They have had an adverse effect, suppressing independent human thought and making it impossible to lead a free, though humble life. This situation of the modern three great monotheistic religions is reminiscent of the conditions when Jesus Christ criticised learned men and Pharisees.

Human existence is not subject to laws and commandments. Jesus Christ taught that commandments are for people, and they are not the most important and indisputable rules of behaviour, but should be perceived as tools. The basic ethics advocated in the Ten Commandments of Moses and in the Twelve Commandments of Muhammad are included in the binding legal system, so they have to be obeyed. Other proscriptions should be changed in every way, according to the wishes of a particular community.

Apart from the basic moral rules, there is no such thing as absolute morality. Depending on the epoch, the development of scientific civilisation, and changes in lifestyles, it is good to be able to make a choice as to what should be accepted and what should be rejected. A true religion teaches only about pure love, and love means the coexistence of all people. We should not allow ourselves to be bewildered with doctrines and words. We must lift our eyes above one fictional point and take a place from which we may see ourselves in our glory.

We have discussed the monotheistic religions. It is now necessary to mention the characteristic features and negative impact of Buddhism.

There is a lot of idolatry in Buddhism. The clergy is hierarchical, and the variety of real and fictional persons can make a person dizzy. These include Greek gods, Gandhara gods, and Hindu gods as well as Buddhist gods. Perhaps that is why, in contrast to three major monotheistic religions of Semitic people, Buddhism did not develop the part of the soul which expresses itself through high feelings, such as piety, dignity, soulfulness, nobility, and purity. Borders which are designated in it are thin, and it is only a chaotic accumulation of various elements. Perhaps that is why, there were not many conflicts in the history of Buddhism.

Approximately 2560 years ago, in the town of Kapilavastu, in a part of ancient India that is now Nepal, Buddha (Siddhartha Gautama) was born. At the age of twenty-nine, he left his home to devote himself to asceticism and meditation, which allowed him to become enlightened. When he was thirty-five, he started dwelling in Northern India and propagated his teachings until he was eighty. One day, as Buddha pondered the fact that people did not understand how his soul had changed after experiencing enlightenment, an evil spirit appeared to him and said, "They do not understand you, that is for sure! Abandon your useless trouble, there is no other world."

Buddha asked, "If it is the truth, from which world you speak to me?"

And the evil spirit disappeared. Then, it is said, Buddha saw Brahma, who asked him to "explain Dharma to poor and suffering people".

Just like Jesus Christ, Buddha also fought with Satan for forty days in the desert.

In contrast, according to the Book of Exodus, soon after Moses' encounter with God on Mount Sinai, while he was meditating in mountains, the Israelites were tempted by evil spirits and broke harsh bans and worshipped a golden calf. We are told in Exodus that when Moses discovered what happened, in anger he punished all engaged people.

Whenever good comes into existence, it is fought against by evil. That is why spreading truths is not a simple task. Still, we must not close our eyes and pretend not to see influence of evil. Buddhism not only does not understand the existence of evil and evil spirits, but since the very beginning, it was not aware of it.

I am going to write some words about the Dhammapada, a Buddhist scripture that is believed to pass Buddha's teachings in the most comprehensible way (the title means "truth", and the whole set is in a form of conversation with Buddha). It is also recognised as one of the oldest Buddhist writings).

First of all, the Dhammapada criticises the caste system, which was deeply rooted in Hindu society, and teaches the equality of everyone before the law. If we compare it to the social norms of the time in which it was written, this was a shocking and revolutionary thought.

The Buddhist notion of "impermanence of all complex phenomena (anicca)" teaches that, although all forms of life keep changing, being born and dying, life as such remains immortal, changing its outside layer.

The Buddhist notion says that "there is no permanent soul (anatman)" means that four types of human suffering—birth, ageing, illness, and dying—are united and in compliance with the doctrine. One must work out a form of existence that crosses all aspects of suffering and is devoid of egoism. What is more, Buddhism also teaches that it is necessary to acquire the law of nature as one's own, taking the harmony and wisdom of the nature, following the way of the golden mean, staying face-to-face with endless space and accepting its magnitude to one's own heart. It also encourages the idea that human life should serve others, and at the end of the day or whenever it is possible, everyone should consider their own thoughts and acts and ask whether they were used properly in our life, work, and relations with others.

Practices of the Noble Eightfold Path, which are the way to enlightenment:

Right opinion:	Developing a right opinion, without being distracted by other matters
Right thinking:	Preserving pureness of thought on the basis of a right view

Right word:	Talking with words full of love and care
Right deed:	Taking only proper actions
Right life:	Leading the right life
Right aspiration:	Making efforts only for the right issue
Right concentration:	Keeping undisturbed thoughts
Right meditation:	Properly practicing meditation

The main aim of the Noble Eightfold Path is to lead a life according to the above mentioned rules so as to remove from the pure heart all mental impurities and free it from earthly desires. This makes it possible to reach the state of the internal, transparent, glowing light—the real I. This state of concentration and appeasement of mind enables one to experience Nirvana. Buddhist practices are the way to dispose oneself (muga) and the way that leads to absolute understanding (taiga).

When asked about the essence of Zen, master Ikkyū Sōjun[7] referred to Gatha of Seven Buddhas[8]:

Do not do evil

Practice good

Clear your mind

This is teaching of All Buddhas.

---

[7] Ikkyū Sōjun (1394-1481): outstanding Japanese master of Zen
[8] Gatha of Seven Buddhas (in Japanese, Shichi Butsu Tsūkaige)

This means that it is necessary to abandon all evil, practice only good deeds, keeping the mind in purity and peace, which is the commandment of all Buddhas. In this way, the teachings of Buddha were explained in a comprehensible way, communicated with a proper depth and by use of a common language.

The teachings of Buddha were written for the first time in the 1st century AD, approximately 380 years after his death in the territory of Sri Lanka.

In approximately 100 AD, in the northwest of India, the school of Pure Earth was born, according to which it was not crucial to follow harsh commandments. It was enough to invoke the name of Amithaba[9] to be reborn in the Western Paradise [10], while the Hokke school[11] claimed that all living creatures may be enlightened. This was the beginning of the development of Mahajan Buddhism, which teaches that through own practices we should strive to save others, postulates the practising of faith while leading a normal life, and states that before Buddha there were other, older Buddhas.

Later, after the birth of Christ, holy Buddhist writings came from India to China by the Silk Road, and between the third and the fifth centuries, the following were translated:

Mahaprajnaparamita Sutra

Lotus Sutra

Vimalakirti Sutra

Sukhavativyuha Sutra

---

[9] Amithaba: Buddha of Unlimited Light
[10] Western Heaven: land whose ruler is Amithaba
[11] Hokke school: later called Nichiren

Avatamsaka Sutra

Mahajana (main Buddhist writings)

In the second half of the third century, Vajrayana Buddhism also appeared, and sometime between 650 and 700 AD, Great Sun Sutra (Dainichi-kyō), Vajrasekhara Sutra, and the holy Buddhist writings Vajrayana (Buddhism writings in Chinese translations) were formulated.

Zen teachings were passed to China in the sixth century by Bodhidharma from Persia, and during the reign of the Tang Dynasty, a few Zen schools, like Sōtō and Rinzai, were formed. When the sovereign of a Korean kingdom, Paekche, sent as a gift to Japan a statue of Buddha and copies of sutras, Buddhism started to spread around the Japanese islands.

Sutras were created as interpretations of Buddha's teachings, and they coexist peacefully, despite many contradictions. They consist of theses presenting Buddhist thought, prose, and poetry, as well as difficult philosophical theories and rhetoric compositions. They include too many figurative expressions; not only ordinary people, but even monks have trouble comprehending the essence of Buddhism and answering questions about it clearly. The situation is a combination of the Hindu weakness for mysticism and the Chinese tendency for exaggeration.

Japanese Buddhist writings were formulated on the basis of their Chinese translations and by use of specific terminology created by the Chinese, causing them to lose some of their past vitality from the point of view of modern man. They departed from the everyday vocabulary and language system that would be known and understood by everyone. In spite of this fact, they try to pass on all mystical and scholastic values, but an ordinary man will not be able to comprehend them.

This is similar to the situation in Medieval Catholic societies, for whom the Bible remained unknown because it was written in Latin. The first person who translated the Holy Book into a native language was Martin Luther.

The modern Buddhist world must bear the consequences of the fact that since the Kamakura Period[12] it has not made any attempts to refresh, revive, or introduce for everyday use the Buddhist vocabulary. If their religious content is delivered in completely incomprehensible rhetoric, it is no wonder that Buddhist writings are perceived as an empty game of words.

In such a way, Buddhism lost its ability to solve tasks and face the demands of modern times. Researchers are absorbed only in sorting and classifying existing Buddhist teachings; they are not able to deduce even a single new value or function. They act like logicians, whose hands are bound with rules of logic, or who have lost the spiritual abilities to judge or have plunged themselves in the sea of historical research.

According to one of the schools, the school of Pure Land, recitation of Buddhist prayers or pronouncing formulas is enough to be reborn in paradise and be saved. The Cult of Amithaba, which spread from India to China, says that the oriental god of light, Mitra, influenced his character. The school of Pure Land took as its way bringing light to human hearts. This approach made the school a crucial one in times of a low level of culture and a reigning feeling of hopelessness caused by cataclysms, poverty, illnesses and wars. Yet in the present times of the civilisation of science, we must not go

---

[12] Kamakura Period: In Japan, 1185-1333.

backwards in our thinking of a thousand or five hundred years to emphasise the necessity of purity of the soul.

Monotheistic religions take as their starting point an assumption that "I believe, so I give myself", while the basis for Buddhism is the thought "I learn and understand right". While monotheism emphasizes "morality", Buddhism prizes the "state of psyche and the soul". We can say that Buddhism is a religion in which the centre is a placed life, not the concept of God. In spite of differences in value systems, both Semitic monotheistic religion and Buddhism derive from the same source; they only took a different tinge when influenced by the demands of the times, surroundings, temperament of the people, history, cultural background, language differences, and character of those who created dogmas. It resembles dispersion of light in a prism, which is white going out of one source and then takes up seven colours, from indigo to red.

Until we appreciate the fact that we can look at the world from the cultural and religious heritage of the past, and until we feel the real situation of our times, our judgements will remain wrong. Living in the times of Edo[13], Chūki Tominaga, a researcher of Japanese ancient thought and culture, explained in a sensible way that the Buddhist sutras are not true writings of Buddha's teachings. He insisted on the assertion that we are not able to find any sutra that gives Buddha's own words, and this conception is right.

Mahayanistic sutras are expressions of thought of deep content, and they take a form filled with drama, with numerous characters. It would be more correct to define them as artistic works, which present ideology in the form of a great theatrical play. Perhaps a vehicle called "Buddhism" can be driven only by Buddha himself, and when a representative of a school tries

---

[13] Edo: period of time in Japan 1603-1867.

to perform this task, the vehicle starts veering off the road, getting stuck in mud and not able to move, or going to a place from which there is no return.

Would it not be enough for Buddhism, which calls for opening the heart to the harmony and wisdom of nature, and including in the soul a magnitude of the space, to have in the role of the universe all sutras and holy texts with practices of the Noble Eightfold Path and Gatha of the Seven Buddhas? I believe that this way of perceiving the soul, thoughts, and practices suitable for *Zen* Buddhism will endure in the future, not losing its vitality.

In present-day Japan, a common cult and memorialising of ancestors is identified with Buddhism, as are the customs of officiating for the deceased and believing in reaching enlightenment through them. Buddha would consider such teachings and rituals shocking and would describe the belief of these people in their magical power as an awkward absurdity with which he has nothing in common. And probably we cannot find any other developed country where people would believe in such nonsense.

Especially new religious groups, which have come into existence in the present day, find benefit in instilling in their followers a conviction that if they do not worship their ancestors, they will be punished with illnesses, accidents, or other tragedies. They use an unknown world and live off the faithful, inculcating fear in their hearts.

They persuade them that "everything is a result of acts from the previous incarnation. So as not to pass faults from the previous incarnation, we must in the present one do good and pay more money as offering, and then through the devoted heart we will wipe out our sins one by one."

The time has come to realise that we have allowed obsolete thinking about the consequences of our parents' acts or guilt from a previous life to entrap us in the chains of allegedly wiping out our own sins. It seems that only in Asia is such childish thinking, so similar to that of the first beliefs, which explains phenomena with the existence of previous and future incorporations and warns that failing to perform rituals will make the dead angry, so widespread. Juggling such notions as karma, fatality, fate, and destination, the new religions on one hand sip venom to the memory of their followers, on the other, they strive to remove it. During the whole process they order the faithful to pay enormous amounts of money and destroy the harmony of many families. It is all only devil's tricks and stratagems.

When there is a reason, sooner or later a result will appear. If the result is wrong, it must be analysed. It should be considered in scientific and rational terms. It is necessary to think, whether such a situation occurred due to lack of attention, efforts, experience, or knowledge. Maybe the time was wrong, and then consequences must be addressed. Bias and assumptions deeply rooted in the subconscious have a very strong influence on us, so that commonly accepted, modern speech and collections of words do not equal those taken from holy books and Buddhist writings. These are eloquent sermons and teachings preached by monks and priests, difficult to understand, which, just like sutras, sound more mystical and therefore command respect. Yet religion is only a tool. It should be used only to allow people to coexist peacefully and societies to function properly. There is no religion or organisation in which everything is wrong.

Religion still attracts people, talking to their minds and hearts filled with love, slowly implementing feelings of fear, losing the main way and taking its followers far from the right understanding of its essence.

2. NEGATIVE RESULTS OF IDEOLOGIES AND DOGMAS

There are ideologies and dogmas, such as Nazism, communism, religious fundamentalism, and all types of nationalism, that do harm to society. They deprive man of the abilities to reason properly and be flexible in judging. Ideologies and dogmas have caused many wars, murders, and acts of terrorism, forming a long history of humanity, stained with blood. Even now, conflicts and growing or reborn hatred between beliefs and religions are the most serious problems of our planet, just as pollution of the environment, overpopulation, threat of nuclear weapons, and energy are problems.

Our weak human natures allow words to deceive us, and such formed reality is accepted as the truth. Man lets himself be carried by emotions, and that is why he can be deceived by words. His assumptions become fact, truth, and reality. Even if something contrary to such an assumption occurs, the man explains it as an accident, negates it, and tries to justify it, or finally ignores and denies it, at the same time making the assumption stronger. He keeps looking for something universal and dependable, and when finally he finds it, he never lets it go, even if the price is his life. Once he has obtained feelings of stabilisation and safety, he will not allow them to be destroyed. Science strives to eliminate illusions and ascertain reality, but man does not try enough to be able to look at the reality from various points of view. He still lacks the courage to make certain decisions and go one step further from the shell that binds him.

A lot of "thrilling" words functions in ideologies. Man, if he lets himself be taken by ideas, seems to emit voltage from his head and enters into a state reminiscent of a kind of ecstasy or daze. From the philosophical point of view, dogmas are doctrines or religious rules that do not recognise rational critiques. That is why his belief is uncritical, blind, and irresponsible. When a man starts believing in something, he takes the faith as a starting point and tries to fix everything to it. Elements that are proper for him make his faith stronger and are its medium, while those that are in contradiction are ignored, denied, eliminated, and rejected.

Ideologies would not have a reason to exist without pointing out what is right and what is wrong. Whether they were religions, modes of thinking, or commandments, or, like communism, were used for incapacitation and exploitation, our history shows that ideologies have caused the suffering of many people to a degree hard to describe. Communism is an extremely perfidious ideology, which aims to abolish the majority of financiers, confiscate property, reinforce oppression towards the working class, split society by implementing a policy of informing and fear, and finally enable monopolization of wealth in the hands of a narrow group of privileged ones. Reasoning that states that if we survive present difficulties, we will see the day of freedom, when we will be able to use our own potential and financial problems will stop bothering us, proves to be extremely useful. It is similar to faith in the Messiah, which functions in Catholicism. People believing in communism could not free themselves from its chains, until the whole system collapsed in front of them, causing enormous shock. When a man hides in the shadow of some idea, which is comfortable for him and calms him down, and additionally he is convinced that, looking through its lens, he can see reality, he does not know and does not want to realize that the words have deluded him.

It is a great mistake to divide things into parts things that should not be divided. Man has forgotten that names and classifications that were formed as a result of such division are only tools, which do not reflect the real world.

In history, various words were used to define one phenomenon, but now the same word can be understood in different ways, causing conflicts. Science seeks to discover or explain truth by an arduous process of "hypothesis—experiment—proof", and has generally crushed ideologies, even if it took lots of time.

All of us live in a world of our own bias, more or less a micro-cosmos, which cannot be comprehended by anyone from the outside—or even by us. We do not have any other option but to ask questions at every opportunity and see how far can we think independently if such an ability is not taken from us.

3. Properties of functions of the brain

Conviction is reality and truth for the person who holds that conviction, but let us look at how shaping and keeping a conviction is affected by and affects the functioning of the brain.

The brain tries to keep an internal balance, levelling as soon as it is possible all states of disturbance. Some defence mechanisms also have a part in this process, trying to keep balance once it is obtained. Regardless of the conclusion, stabilisation and a feeling of safety are the priority for the brain. That is why it negates and tries to escape a state of imbalance or distorted balance.

Short-term memory takes shape due to an increased number of receptors of chemical substances in synapses, but if they are inactive, the number of precious receptors decreases to the starting point and the memory disappears.

In contrast, long-term memory is not shaped by work of neurons. Instead, it is a sort of physical hard drive of the nervous system, preventing any corrections. In the case of long-term memory, when the number of receptors of chemical substances in synapses is at an increased level for a longer period of time, and there is a state of increased productivity in transmitting signals, genes in the nucleus start working, leading to the synthesis of new proteins. These are used to strengthen multiplied receptors. New synapses are created as well, as long as such a state lasts.

That is why, unless the thinking process experiences a shock or emotional turmoil as a result of an overwhelming incident, from the point of view of brain function, it is unlikely that a change in conviction will occur.

4. Mechanisms of psyche and defence mechanisms

Defence mechanisms are a notion introduced by psychoanalysis that states that all mechanisms that protect our psyche, just like humeral immunity or cellular immunity, form defending systems of our body.

Among defence mechanisms are: denying, suppressing, rationalisation, projection, escape, regression, or reaction forming. These are the most representative ones, which allow us to avoid facing reality for some time. We may remove from our consciousness painful emotions or memories that we cannot accepted, and behave as if nothing has happened (suppression), or we may explain a reality that is difficult to accept by transferring responsibility for our own mistakes or failures to others (rationalisation). When such mechanisms are used persistently or for a long period of time, they may stop the development of the psyche and reaching psychical maturity and may result in mental illnesses, psychosomatic diseases, or personality disorders.

Precise control of situations in which we feel discomfort—when we are nervous, angry, or happy—allows us to catch automatically all the defending mechanisms of our psyches. Weaker and less mature psyches defend more often. If defences are used more frequently, it keeps the psyche less mature, which creates a vicious circle, holding man at a low level. All these mechanisms are an obstacle to right reasoning.

Chapter XI
Personality disorders

Before I write about the main subject of this book, which is the problem of seeing oneself and others from the view of the functions of the real I, I would like to write some words about unhealthy relations between people.

We may say that a man's psyche is a work of art, created by him. Personality disorders are a state in which the base under this work of art is bended, and the colours of its background are dark and gloomy. This condition means that, regardless of all his efforts, a man can be taken back to the starting point, or taken even lower. This can cause self-mutilation or behaviours dangerous to others. Almost all psychic illnesses, such as schizophrenia, psychotic depression, and maniac depression, result from damages of neurotransmitters or receptors, and they are illnesses with a biological dimension, while personality disorders are related to the psyche itself. In a sense, these disorders are illnesses of the real psyche.

Everyone hates himself sometimes, but defence mechanisms or improving humour keep the right balance. The person, who hates and is not able to love himself will not be able to love others. A man with personality disorders will think that he loves another person, yet no matter how much love he gets, he is still not satisfied and keeps making the other person prove his or her love. Such a person can love himself and others only on the basis of love of the other person. Usually it causes repetition of a pattern: The partner gets tired of the behaviour and gradually distances herself, which validates the man's belief that he is not loved and causes him to end the relationship.

No matter how deeply he is loved, a person with personality disorders is not able to believe in the love and experience its power. Because he tries to love himself through the love of others, when he lacks that love, he resembles a balloon without air.

Relationships in which one party wants to receive love only to deafen his own worries, imperfection, empty thoughts, and loneliness not only do not last for a long time, but also continually repeat the same script. Because a man with disorders lacks a true self—love, he is obsessive about proving his value and appearance in the eyes of others. Egoism takes the place of self-love.

Negation and hate towards oneself may be directed against others. Such pathologies may appear in the painfully radical forms of bestial crimes, murders, and maltreatment.

Understanding one's own existence and self-consciousness forms the basis of all human relations and one's views on life and world. Behaviour reflects the quality of the relationship one has with one's own I (both conscious and unconscious). Personality disorders, as an illness of the quality of such relationship, pushes people to distorted behaviour.

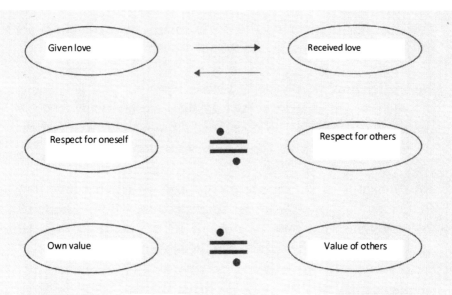

Fig. 11-1 Example of health

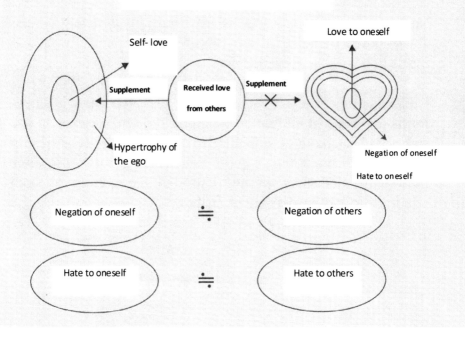

Fig. 11-2 Example of illness

Chapter XII
About Joy

When the real I operates correctly, it is expressed through happiness and joy. Conscious constructing of the psyche in relation to such activity is the only right direction of healthy psychical development, and it is natural.

Fundamentally, human happiness may take only two forms.

The first form is joy felt when, due to full engagement, we have reached our goals and accomplished all desires, or have become a fully actualised person. Such joy strengthens our belief in ourselves, gives the sense that our horizons have broadened and that we grew and allows us to taste the satisfaction that comes from creating ourselves. At the same time, it is a very short-lasting phenomenon, for just round the corner another step awaits us, the step on the way to shaping own personalities.

The second type is the joy of completely using the real I operations. This is the state of unity with others, nature, and all living creatures. Happiness and satisfaction should also be felt in this state. If such happiness accompanies the experience of unity, it is as if it accompanies the experience of love. And in contrast to the rather short-lasting joy resulting from single activities, this one is a living emotion, which can be experienced deeply and for a long period of time, for it is felt on the basis of the psyche being its solid support.

Emotions mean feelings stemming from the feeling of unity with the whole environment or nature, deep feelings that create the colours of the soul scenery and decide its goodness. Emotions are the source of a sense of security, peace, and joy, and are based on the sense of unity. All anomalies of their development are expressed in the aforementioned personality disorders.

Cases of child abuse, parental lack of interest, and over-protectiveness all have a very strong influence on helpless young souls. Distorted characters or the lack of ability to love after losing parents can cause children to fail in their emotional development. When such children reach the age when they start understanding the surrounding reality, despite joy, a sense of security, and peace, they may experience anxiety and corresponding somatic symptoms: irritation, depressive states, mood changes, or a sense of emptiness. Such children are tormented by the emotions that are born when two close people decide to part.

There is also bad joy, or "pleasure". It originates from false and short-term feelings of unity, and is reached through being subjected to influence and domination or using psychical tendencies to masochism and sadism. Feeling pleasure is a base here, much like addiction, and after some time, it requires even stronger stimuli, ultimately causing destruction.

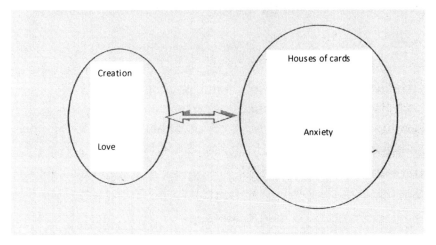

Fig. 12-2

It is important that one not look for the source of happiness, peace, and security outside, but in one's own interior. It is possible only by shaping the psyche, and just as in the case of the source of light of soul, it is the real I. It is crucial to form one's own psyche so that it can be used later in relationships and at work.

When we reach the state at which everything functions ideally, we will be able to influence our environment in the best possible way. Putting it into Buddhist words, the acceptance of the instability of the soul is the most appropriate state for man. It is a state of freedom, when a living organism reaches the strongest level of vibrations. There has never a situation in which any earthly organisms could live independently, in completely isolation from others. All of them are part of a circle, interacting with each other and forming unity, which functions within one organism of harmonised correlation.

So far it is people who endure in a mistake. The tendency to believe magical words and lies is deeply rooted in them. After all, many names and classifiers divide things that should not be divided, and this forms the illusion that they reflect the reality. That is why, with perfection of functions of the real I, which keeps watching the environment, our happiness will grow, we will not be people of a small spirit, but of a great one, and we will be able to form healthy relationships with other people.

Chapter XIII
The unity of everything

I have already written that the starting point for everything is what happens in a man's life, how self-aware he is, and how he understands himself, both in human relationships and with regard to life and his view of the world. A man must ask himself whether he sees himself as a "creature burdened with original sin and karma, as a creature bounded by fate and at the mercy of causality", or as a blessed living creature that radiates with light due to photons of the real I by nature, and whos ego is shaped according to their actions to follow the way of psychological development.

Regardless of his choice, the way he perceives himself automatically causes the man, both consciously and subconsciously, to look at other people in the same way. This is how what he gives to others starts being his own.

Man is able to understand his neighbour only to the degree that he is able to understand himself. It is impossible for him to comprehend fully and understand any other person if he does not know himself. He must start to accept with his whole soul the fact that, from this new point of view, we all are living creatures who radiate with light and who include the source of divinity. It is said that Bodhidharma mediated for nine years facing the wall in order to accept this fact with his all person and feel with his whole soul.

That is why at every opportunity we must return to the base and pave the way from that point, not caring about superficial turbulence at work or in human relationships. The real I, which functions as a glowing, living organism, always acts within the framework of unity of everything, not being separated from the environment. Those who have understood and accepted it at the deeper level of consciousness, and who have been able to shape their psyche in close harmony with the body, according to Buddhist criteria, are living at the level of consciousness which corresponds with the world of Buddha.

We all are unity. Let us leave our selfish I and let us extend a definition of ourselves. Unless we accept fully the new model of understanding others and ourselves, we will not be able to get rid of thoughts, ideas, divisions, and faith that are in conflict with our real I.

It is important to be able to judge properly what is the higher level of consciousness. Unity of everything means that we take care of others and respect them just as we respect ourselves. That what we do for others, we do also for us. Love that we receive is the answer to what we have given our neighbours. When the activity of the real I is completed, man has reached the most favourable state and the deepest joy and peace.

In contrary to that, the man who takes care only for himself, who is interested in his own business, losses and profits, who isolates himself from others, has chosen the worst way of life, where efforts are disproportionately bigger than the harvest. Souls of great wise men have been teaching this for a long time.

Chapter XIV
Soul perfection

The independent formation of the world of the psyche, according to the acting of the real I (photons) is the key to a peaceful and joyful life. It is important to know and properly understand this and to lead one's life on the basis of this understanding, making use of it in everyday matters, both private and professional.

The difference between cognition and complete understanding is huge, and the former is not possible without everyday perfection of the psyche and soul. Soul formation is not only the domain of monks, priests, and pastors. We ordinary mortals should consciously work on ourselves in our everyday, stress-filled lives.

The most important points related to this work are detailed below:

- Every man hides in the depths of his psyche the source of divinity by nature, which is revealed by his acting at the high level the real I—the essence of being—and working very hard to develop his own psyche. However, it depends on the environment, for some differences in development occur.

  The acting of the real I takes the physical form of a bright light in the middle of the head, which becomes even brighter with the development of the psyche, so it can reach such a level of power that it may be mistaken for real light. It is not an abstract ideology. We must remember and be conscious that we are creatures that radiate with light for real.

- Let us take inventory of ourselves: In what moments do we feel joy, anger, irritation, etc., and what is our reflex system? What type of defence functions do we possess? Functions that are used automatically and unconsciously? How were our value system, our faith, and the ideas we profess shaped? What is the rooted power that consciously and subconsciously directs and stimulates our psyche?

  It is not the point to criticise or judge ourselves, but to look at ourselves from different views and angles.

- All words we use, our present thoughts, and our deeds are the decisive factors that co-create our present environment and give it certain consequences.

  Consequences keep asking the man about the meaning of his behaviour, and until their reason is corrected, similar experiences will be repeated inevitably. Let us look consciously at our state every day, and let us try to live in such way that we do not repeat unconscious reactions and involuntary acting from the past.

- Let us not apply modern measurement to life successes or failures. Life is a process that allows us to understand and experience a lot. It is important to what degree such experiences will contribute to our psychical development. Just as one can find a genius in poverty, numerous fools are in clover. Social position and fame are only earthly measures that do not have any meaning from the view of heaven.

Defeat is the mother of success and is its necessary medium. However, success may be a factor causing a fall. The way in which we use the experience has greater meaning, and the answer to the question of whether we succeeded for real or were defeated will only be received at the end of our lives. If we study patiently the history of experiences and mistakes of other people, we can change our lives, and get a new look at the world and our actions, and we will not repeat the same mistakes. Our lives will stop being a chain of subconscious reflexes and repeated experiences from the past.

- The real I is the source of light of the soul, compass, and radar, which keeps pushing a man in the direction of harmony, development, and evolution. As a centre of life, it is the source of joy, peace, innocence, and divinity (exuding the great power of life energy). Because the real I is a spiritual feeling, an emotion of love and unity in itself, it is worth correcting and adjusting our consciousness, deeds, and words to its functioning.

- By doing good for our neighbour, we do good for us. Even if we believe that someone has done something bad to us, it is only the result of our previous activity concerning this person. The shortest way to reach happiness is to make our environment glad, for we gather harvest from what we have done to others. Jesus Christ wanted to pass such information to us, saying, "Whatever you do to your neighbour, you do it to me."

In such a way, we are the union of everything that surrounds us, and this is the real function of the real I. Such thoughts must become automatic and reflexive, until, just like Bodhidharma, we enter them into our subconscious. Supporting and enriching others means doing the same for ourselves. We must not forget that our existence is connected with other people and acts with them.

- Unity of everything does not mean that we and everything around us is the same, but that we are connected with everybody and that we have never parted. Good and evil that we do to others returns to us in unchanged shape. This is why it is a tenet of Judaism and Christianity to "love your neighbour as yourself." Each of us seems to be a separate being, so it is not surprising that we make mistakes easily, but that is why we should repeat to ourselves that in the spiritual world we are unity.

- We should look for the source of the essence and its quintessence, not allowing ourselves to be deceived with words, and also striving to get rid of illusions. We must work out a habit of overall perception.

  We must not escape in faith or in its lack. Whenever we will follow in the direction of faith, we should not lose our ability to reason.

  A man, who is learning psychology thinks that he comprehends the human nature much more deeply, but this is only an illusion. In reality, he has adjusted freshly memorised psychological notions to various situations. If he doubted the specialised terminology and thought about it one more time, he would realise that, honestly, he does not know anything. He only tried to apply the lens of the idea (vocabulary) to the reality.

- Life experiences are used to learn something, broaden horizons of own understanding and deepen them. Even if the man experiences unpleasant consequences, he is not aware and probably even will not think, that his own words, acts and thoughts are bounded with it. Until his responsibility, which he should carry on his own, will burden some fictional creature made in his imagination, some idea, sutra or anyone else, he will feel comfortably, yet his psyche will remain immature, depriving him of a chance for development and progress.

Only when we start thinking, that the only responsibility lies on our side, our inside will be filled with a new wind, giving start for changes.

- Neither faith nor its lack is sufficient to solve all problems, for there is no such thing that can be done without creativity, dexterity, attention, effort, concentration of thoughts, and leading a simple, honest life. Good spirits may help only those who help the others. Let us care about making a little effort every day.

- Let us not feel bounded with the criteria of this world. Living here, we need these criteria, but it is important to recognize some others. It should not be only one empty reference point, but a point of view that allows us to see ourselves and the world as a whole. For example, let us try to look at ourselves and modern reality with the eyes of a creature that came here from beyond the Earth.

- Let us respect people who have different opinions and have made other choices. People used to stigmatise, criticise, persecute, and attack people, states, nations, and races whose opinions and decisions were different from theirs. It may happen that when we meet someone whose views and decisions differ from ours, we start feeling anxiety, as if someone pointed at our imperfections and our identity is shaken. A feeling of unity may be distorted by feelings accompanying all extremities, comparisons, divisions, and conflicts.

A man hides much more in himself than can be judged from his appearance. If we reject bias and superstitions and we will try to realise and understand that different views and choices have their justification, we may discover that they do not differ so much from ours. All differences may be used as a stimulus for further development.

Spiritual evolution may take place in a variety of ways and through making various choices. It is surely divided into many stages.

The functioning of the real I may be defined with the adjectives *grand* and *innocent*. Let us try to keep our soul in a state of innocence. Let us get rid of all bad thoughts and impure ideas, which are unworthy the real I. Let us remember our pure and noble nature, so that such an image of us and others can take root in our heads. We will form the real I on the basis of the above. Only our deep assumptions and behaviour according to the real I have power that allows us to influence others.

We are innocent, proud, and noble creatures by nature, and we have dignity, which must not be violated. Understanding this fact should help people from our environment reach a higher level of consciousness.

Chapter XV
Holy books and their future

We must not forget that both, the New and the Old Testament, and also Buddhist writings, were formed when the fathers of the religions were not present, and were written down by the subsequent generations with scientists and the Church.

In such a context, the Koran is unique, for it was not called to life by posterity, but was written by Muhammad himself, who for twenty years, from the ages of forty-three to sixty-three, was listening to the voice of archangel Gabriel (Dżibril), who sent him revelations and passed the words of Allah (Jehovah, Yahweh).

The Koran occupies a very narrow category of religion, setting up rules regarding every aspect of social life and demanding that they be followed. Nomadic tribes living in the Arabian Peninsula continuously fought each other for their territory, which made them shed blood. Before the birth of Islam, these tribes had never been united and had not created one state. Despite a common cultural background, particular tribes led their own lives, being separate communities. This generally gave their members safety and the chance to survive to. In the name of Islam, the Arab world obtained very detailed regulations concerning ordinary life, religious behaviours, and spiritual life, gaining as a community peace and wealth.

Because such regulations were numerous and too detailed, with the passing of time, they became difficult to adapt to changing times and changes in society. Those who were subjected to them, with their backs to the wall and psychically dominated, lost the freedom to think and act for themselves. When man is in the spiritual world, where an electrical wave called Allah flows at him, his psychics power weakens, and he is not able to feel, think, judge, understand, or find his way for sure. Then the more negative side is seen, which is an obstacle on the way to maturity and spiritual progress.

Due to such a process, the Koran, which in the past was able to create a civilisation no matter what level was reached by art, architecture, medicine, mathematics, and all sciences. Since these cultural levels were higher than other regions, and as the regulations set forth in the Koran stayed at the same low point, the Koran started losing its legitimacy and functionality.

However, in Arab societies devoted to Allah, life based on the Koran is something as obvious as the fact that the Sun rises in the East and sets in the West. That is why the faith system based on its teachings does not lose any of its vitality.

What is more, because of the psychic vulnerability so characteristic of these societies, they have for centuries been falling into bloody conflicts with culturally different regions.

In the sphere of Christianity's influence, the power of the word "God", characterised by a very strong voltage, is gradually weakening, and even in the Judaic society, religion has been pushed to a private dimension and clearly separated from social life.

In countries dominated by Buddhism, its laws became a dead letter a long time ago, preserved only in the form of celebrations and festivals. Buddhist writings, with their ambiguous contents that contradict each other, remain chaotically disordered.

In Buddhist teaching, "enlightenment" means all states, from the smallest one to the completely enlightened, which allow one to experience deep unity of everything and are the beginning of an evolution in understanding oneself and the world. Buddha never said what we should believe. He taught that we should find support in the law. He realised a program of his own development, enhanced through science and self-improvement, which led to enlightenment and reaching happiness.

When a cult of the god Mitra was born in the Orient and came to India, spreading faith in Amitabha, it originated changes that could not be imagined by Buddha himself, for schools worshipping Amitabha and those that based their faith on the Buddhist writings started to form. Buddha taught that we should "understand the universe as Buddhist writings". The word *zen*, which in sanskrit is pronounced *dhyana,* means meditation, and is one of the most important practices taught by Buddha, whose sense must be properly understood.

Zen is a process during which all rooted stereotypes, value systems, and self-consciousness must be set in the daylight and verified, and finally everything must be eliminated from them which is impossible to be subjected to the activities of the real I. And that is why it is said that it enables us to meet the Lord (the real I). *Zen* allows us to realise one more time that everything is unity, and despite the fact that it resembles a religion, such a practice allows our little I to discover the great, wide, and free I, and then to build it in us (Fig. 15-1).

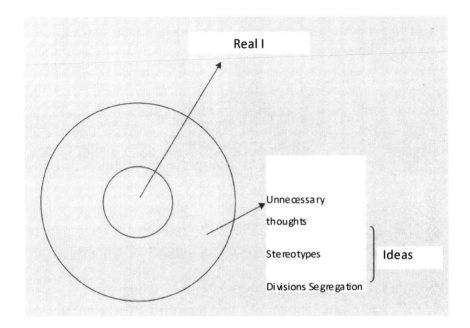

Fig. 15-1

Man has always rejected, negated or ignored people of different views, value systems, races, states, or religions. And yet, he belongs to a particular place and lives with a certain cultural heritage that determined the whole religious system and faith that was instilled in him even before he was able to comprehend its meaning. Most men did not obtain their faith consciously after difficult spiritual searching.

Islam considers Noah, Abraham, Moses, Jesus, and Muhammad to be the five great prophets. The genealogical line of Semitic prophets endured analysis of their revelations. The texts were made modern, adjusted to particular times, their demands, intellectual level, and standards were changed, and mistaken interpretations were corrected. In such a sense, all holy books remain incomplete. There is no such thing as the only book. The record of revelations written by Muhammad also needs to be updated.

Updating does not mean simply correcting or deleting fragments that were the source of misinterpretation, but also eliminating fragments that, with the passing of time, stopped being useful or became an unnecessary burden, and strengthening those that function well. New transcripts in modern language should be added, and expressions should be used that will touch the souls of people living in particular times. Just like a snake, whose moulting is a condition of survival, a religion will rot without the regular shedding of skin and updating. This may be the reason for new conflicts. Apart from common love and support based on a great respect for life, in no religious school is there any other absolute and universal teaching or ethical rule.

Yet both religion and ethics are only tools, which must be used skilfully so that society, family, and the spiritual world function well and preserve harmony. We must not allow others to treat us like slaves, or to exercise control over us.

In holy books of every epoch, whether they were Buddhist, Hindu, or any new religion's writings, the truth has constantly changed the way it is expressed, to free people from incorrect reasoning and to cut chains of misunderstanding from people's hearts. This does not diminish in any way the meaning of holy books and does not offend them. It is untrue that only members of religious schools and people who believe will obtain blessings, luminosity, and care. The truth is that no Buddhist writing or holy book is the only one, nor does it have the final and highest value.

Using Albert Schweitzer as our example, we should strive to fulfil the ideal that the highest ethical standard should be respect given to life (its care and protection). To this end, we should carefully study every Buddhist writing, the Bible, and all holy books of particular religious schools, and then choose the most appropriate fragments. We will be able to see how a great part of these books is used only to enhance the authority of the Church, deifying and adding mysticism to creators of particular religions, and also to increase respect for the holy books themselves and give them a divine character. In the present civilisation of science, these books have not only lost their significance, but are also an obstacle on the way to happiness and spiritual development.

In times of ignorance and superstitions, holy books were used to instil fear of God in people, reinforcing the idea that they are burdened with original sin and karma, so as to strengthen moral rules in them. However, at present, on the basis of new, scientific facts, man is able to understand himself better and more deeply, is able to look at superstitions and illusions from a scientific viewpoint, and can learn and strive towards enlightenment through science.

In olden times, there was no holy book that could be analysed; the books were spread around the world. It was commonly accepted that religion must not go hand-in-hand with science, and when contradictions separated them, religion was seen as superior, so science was completely ignored and could not be used.

There are countless planets, billions of stars, and hundreds of milliards of galaxies. Thus there is no such place as the centre of the universe; each of them reflects its entirety. In space, there are countless living organisms. The conviction that only Earth could give birth to intelligent creatures is proof of man's ignorance and geo-centricity. There will be a day when man boards an object similar to a UFO that flies on the basis of the control of gravitation and magnetic forces, and will go into the space. In this future time, man will start acting according to the spirit of science and will draw on the knowledge of many people, regardless of how different from him they may be. He will have to edit his holy books, because their disagreement with science will be obvious, and the forms of expression used in them will also be changed.

Evolution has strengthened life, because living things had to face challenges in the environment and adapt its functions to survive. If holy books and their accompanying detailed laws, commandments, and faith systems were not ordered and reformed, they would no longer be able to exist.

In the future, holy books will put the universal rights of the soul in the first place and will not be in opposition to the scientific point of view.

Conclusion

At present, the pollution of our environment is rapidly worsening, posing a threat not only to man, but also to every living creature. In this respect, there have never been such wretched times as now. Everyone is at the same time a perpetrator and victim. Because this problem has been caused by collective action, it can be solved only through cooperation and common consciousness-raising. These are times when a single Messiah cannot do anything.

All problems, such as weapons trading, overpopulation, pollution, poverty, and energy come down to money. For sure one of the biggest causes of the problems mentioned above is overpopulation. There are forces that have tried to enslave man's spirit, by means of religion and faith. These forces try to keep him at a low level of consciousness so that they may gain power over him. We must not forget that there are also powers that try to make man dependent, forcing him to cause wars, manipulating him with currencies, shares, and investments, and finally trying to control him in this way.

I hope that this book has made people think about questions of consciousness and faith and has suggested a view of man that is both new and known for a long time. Finally, I hope this book contributes to solving the above-mentioned problems.

If we try to look at the Earth through the eyes of aliens, we will find out that the state of our modern times is very serious. Just like the human body, which is doomed for death, our psyches may consider reality only on the level that is comprehensible for it. If, after reading this book, the reader decides that my interpretation of these issues is limited by my own low level of comprehension, I apologise.

Bibliography

Brennan, Barbara, *Hands of Light*, ed. Kawade Shobō Shinsha

—Chino Yūko, *Door to heaven*, ed. Tama Shuppan

—Drane John, *Introduction to the Old Testament*, ed. Kōdansha

—Gheorghiu Constantin Virgil, *Muhammad's life*, ed. Kawade Shobō Shinsha

—Greene Brian R., *Elegant space*, ed. Sōshisha

—*Illustrated book about physics*, ed. Sūken Shuppan

—*Book of Islam*, ed. Gakushū Kenkyūsha

—*Small encyclopaedia of physic*, ed. Sanshōdō

—Meier Eduard Albert, *Contacts with Pleiades*, ed. Tokuma Shoten

—Murata Masao, *Flying saucers and pseudoscience*, ed. Byakkō Press

—Newman Frank, *Universal of Silver Birch*, transl. Kondō Kazuo, ed. Heart Shuppan

—*Newton*, Newton Press

— Satō Katsuhiko, *Enigma of 96% of the space*, ed. Jutsugyō-no Nihonsha

— *Christian dictionary*, ed. Iwanami Shoten

— *Wikipedia, the free encyclopedia*, etc.

About the Author

Tadataka Kimura was born January 27th, 1954 and lives in Fukuoka, where he practices medicine. A graduate of the Sapporo Medical University (Hoddaido Prefecture), he has experience in clinical treatment in Japan and the United States (internal medicine, emergency medicine, psychiatry, psychosomatic medicine).

At present, Dr. Kimura is the head of the Kasuga Hospital in Kitakyushu.

About the Book

Imagine you are a fish. What do you know about life on the ground? Nothing. You are limited to your own environment. Being a human being, what do you know about the soul or other worlds which coexist with our reality, which is closed in five senses?

In spite of the fact that in our reality deals with the subject of the spiritual world, the existence of the spiritual body and the science of dying are met with prejudices or at least with indifference, the Japanese thinker Tadataka Kimura revolutionizes the old views about man and his consciousness. He explains the origin of our bodies, convinces us to believe in the existence of the soul, and helps in discovering a new understanding of man and his ego.

"The truth of the soul" is a life guide for people, who live in endless row of contradictions, not knowing which way to follow. It is a well of knowledge for those, who wants to enter the path of internal development. This is a book for those, who looks for understanding with the surrounding world.

The psyche is our own work of art. Let us give it a beautiful shape.

Lightning Source UK Ltd.
Milton Keynes UK
UKOW04f2110030316

269561UK00001B/99/P